The Nazi Revolution

PROBLEMS IN EUROPEAN CIVILIZATION SERIES

The Nazi Revolution

Hitler's Dictatorship and the German Nation

Revised and Edited by
Allan Mitchell
University of California, San Diego

D. C. HEATH AND COMPANY

Lexington, Massachusetts   Toronto

Cover: Hitler rides triumphantly through Asch, the first Sude-
ten German town, October 3, 1938. (Wide World Photos)

Published simultaneously in Canada.

Printed in the United States of America.

International Standard Book Number: 0-669-20880-9

Library of Congress Catalog Card Number: 89-80515

10 9 8 7

Preface

This is the third edition of an anthology that was first edited in 1959 by John L. Snell. His untimely death prevented Professor Snell from completing a projected revision, which I was then asked to undertake in his stead. By that time, in the early 1970s, scholarship on the Nazi period had made enormous strides, and the second edition was consequently far different in structure and content from the first.

Now another fifteen years have passed. The tempo of research and writing about Nazism remains astonishingly rapid. Accordingly, this new version has been substantially altered and updated once more. I have retained the topical structure on the pedagogical grounds that it readily permits a critical discussion of coherent themes. But a large number of the individual essays and excerpts used in the second edition have been replaced by more recent publications.

Perhaps it is well to explain briefly the criteria of selection. Part I has been totally changed to reflect current debates about the continuities and discontinuities of German history. The scholars represented here are much less concerned than an earlier generation about deciphering "the German mind." Rather, their attention is focused on the social patterns and political currents that led to the Nazi seizure of power in 1933. Part II concerns the personality of Adolf Hitler. Fascination with the twisted and compelling figure of the Führer is as great as ever. Yet there is a limit to how deeply a single dead man's psyche can be explored; the rest is speculation. I have therefore retained this material intact as it appeared in the second edition, both because this theme was already well covered there and because little of note has been added to it. Part III treats the industrial, religious, and military elites of the German state. How the Nazis were able to harness the political machinery of modern government, and thereby to seduce or throttle any potential opposition, is still a subject much studied by serious historians. Part IV of this anthology is, for good reason, the one most completely transformed. The explanation is simple: social history has been the most active sector of research during the past several decades. Hence it is now possible to include excellent accounts of youth, workers, women, and Jews under the Third Reich. Such topics have lately been explored in more depth than ever before, and we may now examine these findings with some confidence in their soundness.

All in all, this volume is vastly different from the previous two editions that appeared under the same title. In a furiously active and rapidly changing world of scholarship, it could hardly be otherwise. For her expert editorial assistance in helping to contain so much energy between two covers, I want to thank Helene Carol Brown.

A. M.

Contents

Chronology of Events

1871	German Empire (Second Reich) founded.
1889	Adolf Hitler born in Austria.
1907–14	Hitler's Vienna and Munich years.
1914	World War I begins.
1918	World War I ends German (Weimar) Republic established.
1919	Treaty of Versailles signed. Hitler joins German Workers' Party (later NSDAP, or Nazi Party).
1922	Mussolini seizes power in Italy.
1923	France occupies Germany's Ruhr District after German default on reparations payments. Hyperinflation in Germany wipes out savings of most middle-class families. Failed Beer Hall Putsch in Munich (November) leads to Hitler's arrest and imprisonment.
1924	Hitler writes *Mein Kampf* and is released from prison.
1924–30	Relatively prosperous period in Germany.
1927	Ban on Hitler's speeches is lifted.
1928	NSDAP receives 2.6 percent of votes in elections for Reichstag.
1929	Stock-market crash on Wall Street marks onset of Great Depression.
1930	NSDAP receives 18.3 percent of votes in elections for Reichstag.
1931	Collapse of Creditanstalt Bank in Vienna plunges Germany into financial crisis and depression.

1932   Hitler runs second to Hindenburg in presidential election; NSDAP becomes largest German party with 37.4 percent of votes in Reichstag elections.

1933   Hitler becomes chancellor (January).
Reichstag fire and Enabling Act pave way for establishment of the Nazi dictatorship (February–March).
NSDAP declared only legal political party in Germany (July).
Secret German rearmament begins.

1934   "Blood purge" of Röhm and SA, as well as of other opponents (June).
Nazi coup in Austria fails (July).
Hindenburg dies; Hitler becomes Führer (August).

1935   Saar district returns to Germany after plebiscite (January).
Germany begins open rearmament in violation of Versailles Treaty.
Anglo-German agreement permits Germany to rebuild navy.
Nuremberg Laws define Jews' degraded status in Germany.

1936   Rhineland remilitarized (March).
Four Year Plan marks onset of economic planning for war.
Olympic Games in Berlin.
Civil war erupts in Spain, in which Germany aids Franco's Nationalists (July).
Hitler and Mussolini announce "Rome-Berlin Axis" followed by the Anticomintern Pact (Germany, Italy, and Japan).

1937   Hitler reveals plans for systematic conquests at secret meeting with military leaders.

1938   Germany annexes Austria (March).
Czechoslovak crisis and Munich conference lead to German annexation of Sudetenland (September).
Kristallnacht marks the beginning of violent persecution of German Jews (November).

1939   Germany occupies Bohemia-Moravia; Slovakia becomes a German puppet state (March).

Franco triumphs in Spanish Civil War (March).

Hitler-Stalin pact (August).

Germany invades Poland, precipitating World War II (September).

1940   Germany conquers Denmark, Norway, Low Countries, and France (March–June).

Battle of Britain (June–September).

1941   Germany conquers Yugoslavia and Greece (April).

Germany attacks Soviet Union (June).

Japanese attack Pearl Harbor and Germany declares war on the United States (December).

1942   Mass extermination of European Jews begins.

Germany fails to take Suez Canal (March–November).

Battle of Stalingrad marks turn of tide against German army in Soviet Union (September–November).

Allies invade North Africa (November).

1943   Allies begin massive air raids on German cities.

Allies invade Italy; Germans rescue Mussolini (July).

1944   Allies invade France (June).

Attempt on Hitler's life fails; anti-Nazi conspirators are purged (July).

German counterattack on western front fails (December).

1945   Allied armies cross the Rhine and Soviet army besieges Berlin (March–April).

Hitler commits suicide (April).

Third Reich collapses (May).

Surviving major Nazi leaders are tried at Nuremberg, and most of them are executed (November).

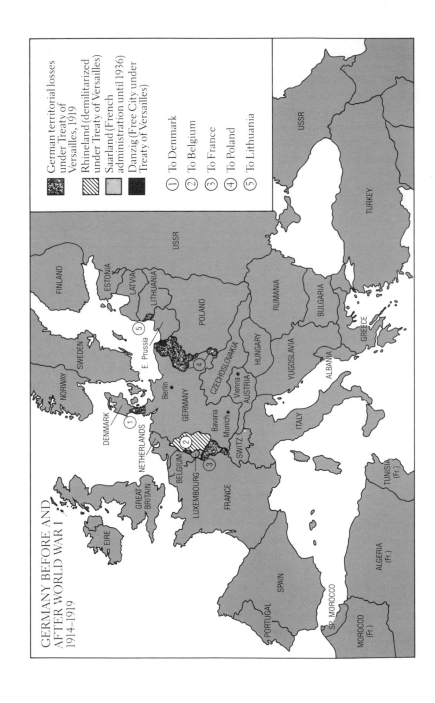

GERMANY BEFORE AND
AFTER WORLD WAR I
1914–1919

German territorial losses
under Treaty of
Versailles, 1919

Rhineland (demilitarized
under Treaty of Versailles)

Saarland (French
administration until 1936)

Danzig (Free City under
Treaty of Versailles)

① To Denmark
② To Belgium
③ To France
④ To Poland
⑤ To Lithuania

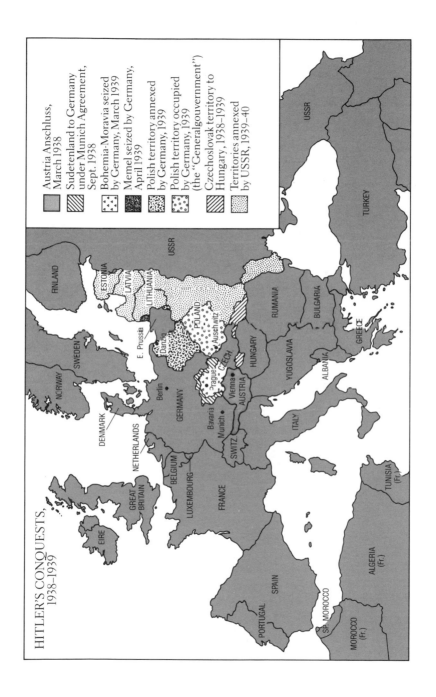

HITLER'S CONQUESTS,
1938–1939

Austria Anschluss,
March 1938

Sudetenland to Germany
under Munich Agreement,
Sept. 1938

Bohemia-Moravia seized
by Germany, March 1939

Memel seized by Germany,
April 1939

Polish territory annexed
by Germany, 1939

Polish territory occupied
by Germany, 1939
(the "Generalgouvernement")

Czechoslovak territory to
Hungary, 1938–1939

Territories annexed
by USSR, 1939–40

Introduction

The title of this anthology announces one of the most extraordinary subjects in all of history. In one sense, German National Socialism was only an episode, lasting in Europe as it did for barely a decade; but in another, it was both a final legacy of the entire nineteenth century and a terrifying symptom of the twentieth. No phenomenon in recorded experience ultimately occupied the energies of so many humans or ended in such extensive devastation. Short of a complete atomic holocaust, our world is unlikely to witness anything comparable ever again.

Although Nazism can thus be perceived as a universal event, or as the most strident example of a fascist epidemic that has infested all of Western civilization, the focus here is deliberately confined to the national context of Germany following the First World War. After all, there is only limited value in speculating about some totalitarian typology until specific instances have been understood as the product of a certain time and place. The chronological distance between our own time and the Nazi years is now sufficient for such comprehension to be possible.

Lamentation is not explanation. Only a few souls wandering somewhere on the sunlit uplands of idiocy could suppose that Nazism was other than an outrage. Yet to denounce Nazism is simply to express a kind of elementary morality; it is not to engage in historical criticism. If we are to begin to penetrate the historical reality, we must ask, and attempt to answer, a number of complex and disturbing questions for which a moral standard provides no absolute guide. We are obligated to regard Nazism with a certain scholarly detachment—which need not be equated with moral indifference—in order to take a more searching look beneath the polemics of years past. This volume is intended to raise such questions and to provide a basis for formulating some of the answers.

Already we can locate at least four perceptible tendencies toward a change of attitudes and interpretations among professional historians:

1. They are inclined to concentrate less on the collective guilt of an entire people and more on structural explanations for the advent of Nazism in Germany. Interest has shifted away from a search for the general intellectual origins of National Socialism to a closer study of the mechanics of the Nazi seizure and exercise of power.

2. At the same time, a deeper research has begun into the individual and collective psychology of those who participated in or were directly responsive to the Nazi movement in Germany. New techniques of psychobiography and psychohistory have raised different problems about the motivation of Nazi leaders and their followers.

3. Greater attention has been devoted to the social thrust of Nazism. Both the immediate and enduring effects of dictatorship on German society have increasingly come under scrutiny in an effort to evaluate more precisely the elements of continuity and change.

4. A subtle but significant alteration has occurred in analysis of the force with which Nazism overcame the possibilities of resistance within the German nation: the leading question has become not so much Was it inevitable? as Was it avoidable? That is, historians have come to adopt a less metaphysical and, as a rule, a less ideological approach toward the problem of National Socialism.

The articles and excerpts collected in this book should illustrate these trends in historiography. They have been selected with this aim in view, and not simply to create an artificial juxtaposition of issues that must be debated in terms of stark either/or alternatives. Dialectical formulations can seldom be resolved categorically in one direction or the other. There is no valid history without nuance, only partisanship. Yet neither can the reader hope to escape responsibility for personal judgment by retreating into a bland objectivity. Some opinions are better than others; and all conclusions have been more or less well conceived. In this regard, it is appropriate to reiterate an admonition of the late John L. Snell from the introduction to the original edition of this volume:

> *Realization that the ideal of absolutely "objective" truth cannot be achieved should lead neither to opportunism nor to despair, but to a more critical, wiser, and therefore more realistic striving to achieve it. It should lead to the study of as many serious approaches to truth as can be found in varying historical interpretations of important events.*

History does not speak for itself. It is articulated only by individual historians and their critics.

The Nazi Circus. Hitler receives the adulation of the crowd upon his arrival in Nuremberg for the Tenth Nazi Party Congress in September 1938. (UPI/Bettmann Newsphotos)

The Nazi Movement and German History

Variety of Opinion

Many threads of development can be traced to the fact that Germany had never experienced a successful bourgeois revolution.

Hans-Ulrich Wehler

The real strands of continuity across the divide of the First World War can best be followed if we look at what did happen in Imperial Germany rather than at what did not.

David Blackbourn

Support for the NSDAP was not uniform and was influenced by the same factors which determined support for the other parties.

Geoffrey Pridham

Unlike their more established rivals, the National Socialists were never content to anchor their movement along traditional lines of social, religious, and regional cleavage that had structured the German party system since its formation in the last half of the nineteenth century.

Thomas Childers

Hitler became Reich Chancellor. His appointment was quite unnecessary.

A. J. Nicholls

We begin with an examination of the peculiar course (Sonderweg) *of German history that led to the Nazi seizure of power in January 1933. It is clear that the Nazi movement was a product of that history. Yet it is also true that a culturally great and complex nation like Germany contained many other contending elements. Why, then, did that one prevail?*

Hans-Ulrich Wehler *draws a straight line from the autocratic regime of Otto von Bismarck, established in 1870, to the onset of Nazi dictatorship. He sees Germany as a land without a democratic revolution, and he emphasizes an unbroken tradition of elitism that allowed modernization but maintained the iron discipline of the imperial state until the military defeat of 1918. Thereupon the old political leadership was temporarily displaced, but the economic and social power of the elites remained unshaken. They merely resorted to more clever manipulative strategies during the unstable interim of the Weimar Republic (1918–1933). Meanwhile, Wehler argues, genuine democratic reform was blocked and outdated reactionary institutions remained in place. When the crisis of the Great Depression struck Germany with full force about 1930, therefore, the Republic was unable to cope and the Nazis stepped forward. In all of this, Wehler stresses, there was a distinct continuity.*

David Blackbourn *takes exception to Wehler's categorical portrayal of political manipulation by the old elites, and he challenges an all-too-neat theory of continuity. He charges Wehler with overstating the peculiarity of German history by assuming that it deviated from a "normal" path of democratic development. In reality, Blackbourn contends, Germany resembled other Western countries in its general tendency toward a modern bourgeois industrial capitalism. In this respect the only difference was that Germany went farther — ultimately, much farther — in the direction of fascism. Thus Nazi Germany was, in Blackbourn's opinion, not an exception but an exaggeration.*

Geoffrey Pridham *writes about the early days of the Nazi party, when it was an obscure rightist splinter group in the southern German state of Bavaria. There, in 1923, Adolf Hitler and his cohort first burst onto the scene during a bizarre attempt to bring down the Weimar Republic by executing a military* putsch *in Munich. The inglorious failure of that episode brought Hitler a certain notoriety and a chance to rethink his tactics. From this base, Pridham explains, Nazism gradually moved northward as it developed dynamic leadership and mass appeal. Once the Weimar Republic began to founder in the economic and political turmoil of the early 1930s, Hitler's party was thus able to overcome traditional constraints in Bavaria and elsewhere and to promise a new national order.*

Thomas Childers *analyzes the electoral strategy of the Nazi party, which solicited votes from all segments of German society and attempted to transcend the narrow bounds of region, confession, and class. While he recognizes Nazism's obvious appeal to adult lower-middle-class males, Childers shows that it also made conspicuous inroads with the affluent bourgeoisie, youth, women, and even some blue-collar workers. Hitler's party had the least success among those social groups that already had stable political organizations with which they strongly identified: Catholics who voted for the Center party (Zentrum) and industrial workers who supported either the Social Democratic party (SPD) or the Communist party (KPD). Childers sees the Nazi movement (NSDAP) as a party of protest that was anticapitalist, antimodernist, and to its core anti-Semitic.*

A. J. Nicholls *describes the final months of political crisis at the end of 1932, when the Weimar Republic finally collapsed and Hitler emerged as the chancellor. Franz von Papen and Kurt von Schleicher, two representatives of the old elites, unsuccessfully attempted to bail Germany out of difficulty with one last manipulation. At the same time, within the Nazi camp, Gregor Strasser posed a possible alternative to Hitler, whose party showed signs of electoral fatigue and financial exhaustion. Already in his late eighties, President Paul von Hindenburg sought a solution and foolishly agreed to a desperate gamble: Hitler was allowed to enter the cabinet as a minority member, where he might be controlled by his more respectable colleagues. But, as we know, this calculated risk was a mistake; within a few weeks Hitler would sweep the others aside.*

Taken together, these five brief statements enable us to comprehend both the dissolution of republican democracy in Germany and the triumph of Nazism. The two developments were simultaneous but not entirely synonymous. The Nazis realized better than their opponents that a good offense is the best defense, in politics as on the playing field, especially in a game of sudden death.

Hans-Ulrich Wehler

The Case for Continuity

Many threads of development can be traced to the fact that Germany had never experienced a successful bourgeois revolution. This resulted in a lack of questioning and opening up, or at least loosening up, of traditional structures. The unbroken tradition of government by pre-industrial power-élites, the prolongation of absolutism among the military, the weakness of liberalism and the very early appearance of deliberalising measures suggest on the surface a depoliticising of society, but one which deep down favoured a continuation of the *status quo*. The same can be said of the barriers to social mobility, the holding over of differences and various norms between separate estates, which is such a revealing aspect of Imperial Germany, and the essentially élitist character of education. Much of this resulted from the political weakness and defeats suffered by the bourgeoisie in the nineteenth century, and all these factors, which are given here only as examples, had assumed their importance during a phase of historical development which was uninterrupted by a successful revolution. They were further strengthened by the success of Bismarck's policies for legitimising the *status quo*. This achievement did not preclude a partial modernisation of the economy, since after 1848 the strategy of "revolution from above" at first had the effect of strengthening the nascent industrial system. Nor did it rule out other achievements. Technical education was so well organised against the various efforts to resist its progress that the flow of scientific and technological innovations began relatively early on and was subsequently maintained. Many of the big cities profited from the retreat of liberalism's leading lights into local government, as well as from the bureaucratic tradition. It was not by chance that, after the 1890s, German local government, together with its communally-run public services, was regarded as a model by the American "progressives." While it is true that in 1895 more than 170,000 workers, punished as a result of their involvement in strikes, knew what it was to be on the receiving end of a system of class justice, the law nevertheless ensured a high degree of physical safety in the towns and rural districts. This was as true for workers and for members of national minorities, as for other social groups. Anyone who thinks highly of American party democracy should also look at the darker side of life in the United States — at, for example, the jungles of New York's immigrant quarters or the lynch justice of the South, to which for decades after the Civil War at least one Black per day fell victim. Party politics, lynch justice and life in the big cities may not appear commensurable with the above; but any comparing of systems inevitably draws upon positive or negative aspects of each, for which direct comparisons are difficult to find. In the German Empire it was not only discipline and repression which ensured social cohesion — whatever their undeniable effects, both subtle and obvious — but the conditions of everyday life. All protests to the contrary, the majority of Germany's citizens did not find these so oppressive that the crises of the Empire developed into a revolutionary situation before the war.

As regards the ruling élites' ability to adapt to changing circum stances, we must again enquire into the reasons for the system's relative stability, the traditional bases for which have been pointed out several times. We can only say, in the language of modern theory, that "pathological learning" was in evidence in several areas. The retention or introduction of class-based electoral laws, the reaction to fundamental social conflicts and the creation of income taxes, the Zabern affair of 1913 or the belated repeal of the clauses on language in the Imperial Law of Associations in April 1917 — all reveal, even if measured solely in terms of a pure self-interest in upholding the system, such an extreme narrow-mindedness that Bethmann Hollweg's judgement would seem to be borne out. History, his associate, Riezler, recorded, would reveal "the lack of education, the stupidity of militarism and the rottenness of the entire chauvinistically minded upper class." This is what directly paved the way for the revolutionary crisis of 1918. In other areas where the élites endeavoured to hold on to their inherited positions of power, their successes outweighed the risks involved. There is no denying that the system of connections between the nobility, the ministerial bureaucracy, the provincial authorities and the district administrators — who were a veritable pillar of stability east of the river Elbe — created political tensions. But the myth of the bureaucracy's neutrality and the patina of inherited traditions, together with the preference shown to powerful interests, kept these below the danger-mark for a considerable time. Without doubt, the combination of compulsory military service with a social militarism in everyday life, in school subjects and in various organisations, created areas of friction. But the gains made in terms of the stability which these elements helped to achieve more than made up for this friction throughout the period up to and including the first years of the war. In both cases, it was not until November 1918 that the true extent of the population's strong dislike of the bureaucracy and the military could be seen.

Most effective of all, perhaps, were those strategies which, also depending on the ruling élites' capacity to learn, combined an ability to adapt to modern forms of politics and propaganda with, at the same time, a stubborn defence of their inherited positions of power. The unholy trinity of social imperialism, social protectionism and social militarism provides more than sufficient examples of this. In this case of social imperialism, the ruling élites' reaction to industrialisation was closely linked to its usefulness in stabilising the social and political hierarchy of privilege. In the case of social protectionist measures, institutional arrangements of future import, such as state legislation on social insurance, were combined with welfare measures and rights which were not essentially liberal, but reactionary, so long as they led to an increase in the numbers of "friends of the Empire." In the case of social militarism, which was intensively encouraged, privileges of social status handed down from the past were defended by means of modern techniques of political campaigning pursuing carefully thought-out aims. The same is true of the early forms of state interventionism. Even a modern-style pressure group like the Agrarian League reveals quite clearly how this ability to adapt to modern methods of organisation and propaganda was entirely compatible with the continued promotion of traditional interests. All in all the entire process, which Hans Rosenberg has described as "the pseudo-democratisation" of the old agrarian elite, showed an often astonishingly flexible readiness on the part of the ruling élites to move with the times while all the more ruthlessly defending their traditional positions behind the façade.

All these strategies, measures and processes of pathological and ingenuous learning were interwoven. Together with a combination of traditionalism and partial modernisation, they were able, on the one hand, to preserve the stability of an historically outdated power structure over a surprisingly long period. Time and time again they achieved the necessary social cohesion. On the other hand, they added, especially in the long run, to an unmistakably increasing burden. The various interests and traditions thus protected became all the more difficult to reconcile with the growing demands for equality, a share of power and liberation from an increasingly intolerable legacy. Just as the economic successes of German industrialisation threw up enormous social and political problems, so the successful defence of traditional political, social and economic power relationships exacted its price. The costs were all the greater and more numerous as a result. The accumulation of unsolved problems which eventually had to be faced, the petrification of institutions which had outlived their usefulness and were in need of reform and the obstinate insistence on prerogatives which should no longer have been the sole property of the privileged few, pronounce their own judgement on the extent to which the ruling élites were prepared to adapt. So do the continual recourse to evasive strategies and attempts to divert attention from the need for internal reforms, as well as the decision to accept the risk of war rather than be forced into making concessions. In practice, the ruling élites showed themselves to be neither willing nor able to initiate the transition towards modern social and political conditions when this had become necessary. This is not a judgement based on theoretical speculation but on processes which culminated in the breakdown of the German Empire in revolution and the end of the old regime. This hiatus now belongs among the undisputed facts of history and cannot be explained away. It represented the bill that had to be paid for the inability of the German Empire to adapt positively to change.

The fact that this break with the past did not go deep enough and that the consequences of the successful preservation of outworn traditions remained everywhere visible after 1918, accounts for the acute nature of the problem of continuity in twentieth-century German history. Instead of bewailing "the distortion of judgement caused by the category of continuity," in arguments which patently seek to defend the German Empire's record, we should, in keeping with the essential requirements of an historical social science, face up to the problems of continuity and seek to analyse them further, rather than encourage an escapist attitude. This does not, of course, mean we should offer superficial explanations based on the "great men" approach to history (from

Bismarck to Hitler via Wilhelm II and Hindenburg); rather we should investigate the social, economic, political and psychic structures which, acting as matrices, were able to produce the same, or similar, configurations over a long period of time. Conversely, we should also analyse those factors which gave rise to anomalies and discontinuity. The question as to whether, in fact, certain conditions favoured the emergence of charismatic political leaders in Germany should be re-examined against the background of these structures.

In the years before 1945, and indeed in some respects beyond this, the fatal successes of Imperial Germany's ruling élites, assisted by older historical traditions and new experiences, continued to exert an influence. In the widespread susceptibility towards authoritarian policies, in the hostility towards democracy in education and political life, in the continuing influence of the pre-industrial ruling élites, there begins a long inventory of serious historical problems. To this list we must add the tenacity of the German ideology of the state, its myth of the bureaucracy, the superimposition of class differences on those between the traditional late-feudal estates and the manipulation of political anti-Semitism. It is because of all these factors that a knowledge of the history of the German Empire between 1871 and 1918 remains absolutely indispensable for an understanding of German history over the past decades.

David Blackbourn

German Peculiarity
in Question

All national histories are peculiar, but some appear to be more peculiar than others. Few historians of modern Germany, whether native or non-native, can escape awareness of that. Historians of other countries are also engaged in some manner with examining national myths: 1688 and the English genius for gradualism, 1789 and the French revolutionary tradition, Easter 1916 and the Irish nationalist mystique. The work of revisionism, in each of these cases, has frequently been a matter of debunking, questioning the pieties of the myth, and pointing up its paralyzing as well as emancipating features. But post-war historians of Germany have seen themselves presented with a still more daunting task. They have been concerned not just with residual elements of myth, but with explaining why the course of German history led to 1933. . . .

What can be said about these ways of looking at the German past? First, of course, their questions and answers have produced much of the most illuminating work on modern German history during the last decades. In no way has the present essay sought to belittle these achievements. Secondly, these perspectives on the past are clearly not identical with each other. They emerged from different milieus and betray different casts of mind and temperament. In many points of detail and interpretation they would make odd, even incompatible, bedfellows. But there are certain basic questions and answers which they share. They view 1933 as the final outcome of a particular historical continuity; they see that continuity as the product of German peculiarity; and they see a crucial element of that peculiarity in the aberrant behaviour of the German bourgeoisie. While these approaches are therefore neither identical with each other, nor of course the only ones in which modern German history has been discussed, they nevertheless have sufficient common threads and sufficient stature to be worthy of critical attention. If there is a figure in the carpet it is German peculiarity, of which in turn the failure of the bourgeoisie to conduct itself like a "proper" bourgeoisie is a central motif. It is dissatisfaction with this way of looking at things that has prompted the present essay. . . .

I have also questioned the idea of "manipulation" with which historians have commonly described the cynical preservation of class interests (particularly those of a "pre-industrial élite"). This, once again, does not entail denying the elements of political dishonesty which characterized Imperial Germany; but it is easy to misidentify the range of would-be manipulators, and to approach the question of political manipulation itself one-sidedly. I am skeptical of accounts that depict the political process, in Gramsci's words, as "a continuous *marche de dupes*, a competition in conjuring and sleight-of-hand." It does greater

Pillars of the Reich. Hitler is shown at a Nazi party rally in 1934, flanked by members of his staff: (to his left) Julius Streicher, managing editor of *Der Stürmer* (The Fighter), the Nazi party newspaper; (to his right) Rudolf Hess, head of the political section of the party and third deputy of the Führer; Viktor Lutze, head of the SA following Röhm's death; and Heinrich Himmler, head of the SS. (UPI/Bettman Newsphotos)

justice to a complex historical process to recognize that if we are to talk of manipulation at all — and I prefer the term demagogy — we should at least recognize that it was a two-way process which was politically unpredictable and potentially dangerous. This approach need be neither ingenuous nor "populist." The purpose of questioning the idea of manipulation by a particular élite is not to substitute a view that everything happened "from below" (which might be called the populist heresy), or that it happened because of the entry of "the masses" into politics (the older conservative orthodoxy). The intention here has been to try to add the missing dimension to accounts that habitually present the sound of only one hand clapping. Similarly, I have not sought to deny the elements of continuity that link the history of Imperial Germany with the Weimar Republic and the Third Reich. It would hardly be necessary to make such a disclaimer, perhaps, had apologist historians not insisted on portraying the Third Reich as an "accident." The real question about continuity is not "whether" but "in which ways?" I have offered an implicit answer to the second of these questions by suggesting that we examine nineteenth-century Germany itself from a rather different perspective. This arises partly, of course, from a desire that Imperial Germany especially be treated less as a mere prelude to what followed. In terms of continuity, however, this could be put in more positive terms. To return to the opening remarks of the essay, the real strands of continuity across the divide of the First World War can best be followed if we look at what did happen in Imperial Germany rather than at what did not.

Perhaps a final observation is called for on the dangers of complacency, moral as well as historical, if we insist too much on a certain kind of German peculiarity. While he was preparing *Doctor Faustus*, Thomas Mann warned of creating "a new German myth, flattering the Germans with their own 'demonism'." Nearly forty years on, we see this problem at its most acute in the ephemera which has helped to establish the Third Reich as a macabre, but chic, chamber of horrors. That is what Hans-Jürgen Syberberg meant by referring to the Third Reich as "our Disneyland." Historians cannot dismiss this problem with an impatient gesture, for it raises moral implications for their own work. The charge of "trivializing" the Third Reich has been raised in recent acrimonious exchanges between historians of the 1930s, and the general issue is clearly present beneath the surface of the *Sonderweg* debate. My own view is that serious historians are perhaps most likely to "trivialize" modern German history in an involuntary manner: by exaggerated emphasis on the absoluteness of German peculiarity, which indirectly bolsters the morbid mystique of German history. There is a pedagogic, as well as a historical, argument for denting that mystique, just as there is a parallel case for not placing swastikas routinely on the covers of books dealing with twentieth-century Germany. That does not mean that we should write the history of Germany as if it were like the history of everywhere else; only that we should not write it as if it were quite unlike the history of anywhere else. The distinctiveness of German history is probably best recognized if we do not see it (before 1945) as a permanent falling-away from the "normal." In many respects, as I have tried to show, the German experience constituted a heightened version of what occurred elsewhere. This is true of Germany's dynamic capitalism, and of the social and political consequences it generated. It is true of the complex mesh of private and public virtues and vices which were characteristic of German bourgeois society. It is true of a widespread sentiment like cultural despair, and of the crass materialism which unwittingly reinforced it. It is true, I believe — although not all will want to accept this — of the way in which these and other phenomena discussed above combined to produce Germany's exceptionally radical form of fascism. What stamps the German case as distinctive is, of course, the particular, uneven combination of these elements. This is not an attempt to smuggle peculiarity in again through the back door. As we have also seen, this unevenness of economic, social, and political developments was not in itself peculiarly German: Germany was much more the intensified version of the norm than the exception. That it so often appears exceptional probably owes a good deal to the distorting focus of a more acceptable myth — that of a benign and painless "western modernization." There is much to be said for shifting our emphasis away from the *Sonderweg* and viewing the course of German history as distinctive but not *sui generis*: the particular might then help to illuminate the general, rather than remaining stubbornly (and sometimes morbidly) peculiar. That would be less likely to encourage apologetics than to disarm them. It might also enlarge rather than diminish our sense of modern Germany as a metaphor of our times. We recognize the richness of allusion when Walter Benjamin called Paris the "capital of the nineteenth century." We should be similarly open to the full meaning of Germany as the "tragic land" of the twentieth century. Our historical and moral sense of that tragedy is sharpened, not blunted, if we decline to view it solely as the final culmination of German peculiarity.

Geoffrey Pridham

The Roots of Nazism

The Nazi "seizure of power" in 1933 brought a political revolution in Germany, but the relative ease and rapidity with which the Nazis secured control over the state can only be explained in the context of the enduring political crisis of the preceding years. The Weimar Republic had failed to establish its legitimacy making it vulnerable during a time of economic and political upheaval. The Depression of the early 1930s crystallized the weaknesses of its political structure and accelerated the disintegration of its authority. The NSDAP assumed at the same time the role of the main opposition force in the state and infiltrated many different levels of German political life. Although it acted generally within constitutional bounds, the NSDAP nevertheless managed to present itself not only as an alternative government but also as an alternative political system. This distinction became clouded towards the end of the Weimar period, when the Republic became less of a democracy in reality and moved towards an authoritarian régime.

The rise in popular support for the NSDAP within the space of a few years was still phenomenal in spite of all these conditions, for in 1928 it had counted as merely one of a number of small parties in terms of electoral support. The party's reputation at this time was based not on its success in attracting voters but on the dramatic event of the Munich Putsch and the notoriety of its leader as a mob orator. A study of the NSDAP in Bavaria offers many lessons on how the party achieved its success. These may be summarized under the general headings: the character of the NSDAP as a totalitarian movement; the nature and extent of its mass appeal; and the relationship between the NSDAP and the state.

Firstly, the party's rise in prominence in the early 1930s was made possible by the fact that it had already established an elaborate leadership structure and laid the organizational basis for its expansion as a mass movement. The NSDAP emerged from the period of its prohibition after the Putsch in a state of weakness owing to the divisions among its leaders and activists and its limited appeal to the public. Its principal strength then was the figure of Hitler, who had succeeded in surrounding himself with the myths associated with the Putsch by the right-wing opposition to the Weimar Republic. It was already apparent at this stage that Hitler's charismatic leadership was entirely separate from internal party disputes and conflicts over policies and tactics, a factor which remained constant throughout the years of the party's rise to power and proved crucial during the critical months which preceded Hitler's appointment as Chancellor.

The pull of Hitler's *Führer* appeal among his followers was especially strong in Bavaria, where his release from prison late in 1924 soon led to rival party groups dissolving their differences and submitting themselves without question to his control. Hitler encountered less difficulty in reasserting his authority in Bavaria than anywhere else in the country because his party had its strongest roots here, as it had certain "Bavarian" associations which in fact made it less attractive among party circles in Northern Germany and because of the proximity of party headquarters which allowed Hitler to make greater use of direct contact with local party leaders there. But the memory of the Munich Putsch proved to be a double-edged sword. While it enhanced Hitler's image in the eyes of the extreme Right, it also dominated the view of Hitler held by the Bavarian authorities. Their decision to ban Hitler from making public speeches for two years shortly after the party was refounded neutralized the main asset enjoyed by the NSDAP.

The situation appeared stable when the ban on Hitler's speeches was lifted in 1927, but it was nevertheless evident that the NSDAP constituted a different kind of party from the others on the extreme Right of German politics, not to mention the moderate parties in the Weimar Republic. If the NSDAP was most akin ideologically to the Nationalist Party (DNVP), it had more in common in terms of party structure with the Communists (KPD) from whom it borrowed ideas on methods of organization and techniques of mass agitation. The NSDAP and the KPD were similar in their attention to new methods of propaganda, although the former used these more successfully in mobilizing wider sections of the electorate. Both parties would be classified as totalitarian, but the main difference between them was the prominence given to ideology by the Communists and the emphasis on the *Führer* figure in the case of the Nazis.

The "*Führer* principle," which had held the party together during the years of its eclipse in the mid 1920s, now became more elaborately systematized. The changes in organization during 1928–29 involved a rearrangement of departments at headquarters, alterations in the regional structure of the party to coordinate it with the electoral system, as well as a more methodical and centralized approach to party activities. . . .

The continuous emphasis on propaganda activities and electoral success which followed created a momentum of its own among party activists. The image of activism which the party cultivated and its promise of a new kind of involvement in politics accounted for the increasing attraction felt by young people towards the NSDAP. A generational gap emerged between the totalitarian parties — for the KPD was also successful in winning the active support of young people — and the older traditional parties. This momentum furthermore reduced the possibilities of conflict within the party by providing a common focus of activity, although tension and differences were still apparent over adaptation to new techniques in rural propaganda, attempts to initiate a party press and in some cases over the development of specialist organizations. When the momentum lapsed, as during the second half of 1932, the consequences were seen in the rise in internal party tension. Such conflict arose also from Hitler's deliberate policy of "divide and rule" as well as the existence in spite of the party's growing bureaucracy of a state of semi-anarchy with the overlapping of authority created by the proliferation of party offices. All these problems had no adverse effect on the central feature of the NSDAP, namely loyalty to the *Führer*, and in fact the accusation of insufficient loyalty to him was often used in internal party disputes. It was this characteristic together with the party's professional methods of organization and superior techniques of propaganda which distinguished it from conventional protest parties on the extreme Right.

Secondly, the NSDAP was distinguished by the unprecedented

degree with which it attracted mass support. Its achievement could be attributed partly to its successful organization, but the answer must also lie in the nature of its popular appeal. There were two main sources of its electoral support: firstly, the liberal and conservative parties in the towns and the peasant parties in the countryside; and, secondly, the new voters. The NSDAP succeeded largely in attracting the support of the middle classes, although it endeavoured to present itself as an integrative force which claimed to represent different interests in society, a claim strengthened by the flexibility of its propaganda and its development of specialist organizations. The NSDAP came the closest there was in the Weimar period to a "people's party" (*Volkspartei*) appealing across classes and interests. . . .

Support for the NSDAP was not uniform and was influenced by the same factors which determined support for the other parties. The most important of these factors was confession. It is clear from the voting patterns of the NSDAP in Bavaria that support for the party was much higher among Protestants than among Catholics. The confessional factor was evident too at the local level of politics where Protestant and Catholic communities were neighbours in the same area and even cut across economic interests, for the NSDAP faced more problems in winning over the peasantry in Catholic areas than it did in the Protestant areas of rural Franconia. The reason for the importance of the confessional factor was firstly the existence of a strong Catholic party, and secondly the fact that in the case of Bavaria Catholic interests were allied with regional patriotism. There were certain similarities between the Bavarian People's Party and the NSDAP, for both managed to appeal across classes and both were essentially "ideological" rather than interest parties, but the substructure of politics in the traditional region of "Old Bavaria" was weighted in favour of the BVP. This party owed the stability of its vote until 1933 to the active and moral support of the Catholic associations and the Catholic Church as well as to its ability to project its own "fundamental view of life" which offered a form of emotional security in a time of crisis. . . .

Thirdly, the NSDAP's rise to power has finally to be examined with reference to its relationship with the state. The case of Bavaria again throws interesting light on how such a totalitarian party operated in a parliamentary system like that of the Weimar Republic. Hitler had chosen the path of "legality" out of necessity, but this did not exclude the violent element in the Nazi movement for it rather contained it.

Hitler managed to siphon off the energies of the most revolutionary wing in the party, the SA, by using them as fuel for his electoral locomotive. Yet political violence was endemic in German politics then and helped to make a sham of Weimar democracy. It was evident not so much in the form of political assassinations, which had marked the early years of the Republic, as the way in which it intruded into everyday politics — through the existence of party military organizations, and the change in the political atmosphere with the growth of civil warfare during the last critical years of the Republic. Such a state of affairs seriously affected the authority of the Republic and brought about a polarization of politics, which could only benefit a party promising a new form of law and order.

The NSDAP's attitude to Bavarian particularism was to some extent a barometer of its general attitude towards the state. Whereas previously the party had camouflaged its centralist tendencies and sought to take refuge in Bavarian hostility to the Reich, it showed less sympathy for Bavarian susceptibilities once it gained a wide popular following and was no longer dependent on the goodwill of the Bavarian Government. The Reichstag Election of 1930 was an important stage in this development, for electoral success blessed the Nazis with political respectability and made adherence to their cause not merely one of ideological conviction or hostility to the Republic but also one of political opportunism. The party's change of attitude to Bavarian particularism became clear during the summer of 1932, when the government in Munich found itself in conflict with the new Reich Chancellor over his decision to lift the ban on the SA. By this time, Bavaria had assumed a different role in the Weimar Republic. It was no longer the patron of right-wing extremism, as it had been in the early 1920s, and had become now a source of resistance to the growth of authoritarian tendencies in national politics.

Bavaria's importance as an individual state during the political crisis which enveloped Germany in the early 1930s was reduced, however, by the general disintegration of authority in the Weimar state and the dramatic rise in popular support for the NSDAP. The Bavarian Government proved incapable in the face of these developments to resist the Nazi "seizure of power" and was further weakened by its adherence to the conventional rules of politics at a time when they were becoming less relevant. The NSDAP had succeeded in pervading German political life by working within the system, but at the same time it had not lost its essential revolutionary characteristics in the form of its radical energies, its aim to create a new political order and its promise to bring new social élites and a younger generation to the summit of politics.

Thomas Childers

The Party's Electoral Appeal

From its first campaign in the spring of 1924 to the pinnacle of its electoral fortunes eight years later, the NSDAP remained an enigma in German political life. Unlike their more established rivals, the National Socialists were never content to anchor their movement securely along the traditional lines of social, religious, and regional cleavage that had structured the German party system since its formation in the last half of the nineteenth century. Instead, they were determined to transcend those widely accepted restrictions on their potential constituency to become the first genuine party of mass integration in German political history. National Socialist electoral strategy, with its consistent efforts to mobilize support in every sector of the economy, in every occupational group, in every region, and in the major Christian confessions, vividly reflected that ambition. Although the party shifted the emphasis of its campaign strategy after 1928, revising the urban plan and concentrating more pointedly on the middle-class electorate, it never abandoned its efforts to cultivate a broader constituency. . . .

Although the NSDAP succeeded in exploiting the widespread disaffection with the traditional liberal and conservative options, support for the party was unevenly distributed among the different groups of the middle-class electorate. Indeed, support for National Socialism varied in duration and degree and sprang from a wide variety of motives. It

From *The Nazi Voter: The Social Foundations of Fascism in Germany, 1919–1933*, by Thomas Childers. Copyright © 1983 by The University of North Carolina Press. Reprinted by permission.

was, however, by no means confined to the lower middle class or to socially marginal declassés. The nucleus of the NSDAP's following was formed by the small farmers, shopkeepers, and independent artisans of the old middle class, who constituted the most stable and consistent components of the National Socialist constituency between 1924 and 1932. It was among these groups that the fear of social and economic displacement associated with the emergence of modern industrial society was most pronounced, and it was among these groups that the NSDAP's corporatist, anti-Marxist, and anticapitalist slogans struck their most responsive chord. Nazi sympathies within the old middle class certainly intensified and broadened after the onset of the depression, but the persistence of those sympathies even in the period of relative prosperity between 1924 and 1928 strongly suggests that this support did not represent a spasmodic reaction to immediate economic difficulties but expressed a congenital dissatisfaction with long-term trends in German economic and social life. . . .

Although National Socialist sympathies among lower-middle class white-collar employees were less developed than expected, the NSDAP found a surprisingly large following in more established social circles. By 1932 the party had won considerable support among the upper middle-class student bodies of the universities, among civil servants, even in the middle and upper grades, and in affluent electoral districts of Berlin, Hamburg, and other cities. Motivations were myriad, including fear of the Marxist left, frustrated career ambitions, and resentment at the erosion of social prestige and professional security. Yet, while sizable elements of these groups undoubtedly felt their positions or prospects challenged during the Weimar era, they cannot be described as uneducated, economically devastated, or socially marginal. They belonged, in fact, to the established elites of German society.

Just as the Nazis were winning support from elements of both the upper- and lower-middle classes, they also secured a significant constituency within the blue-collar working class. Usually ignored or dismissed as unimportant, the NSDAP's prominent solicitation of a working-class following and its success in the endeavor, were exceptional in the context of German electoral politics. Aside from the confessionally oriented Zentrum, the NSDAP was alone among the non-Marxist parties in its efforts to establish an electorate within the blue-collar population. Even after 1928, the party refused to concede the blue-collar electorate to the left and continued to invest a surprising amount of energy to win working-class voters. Nor were those efforts — which led the traditional bourgeois parties to denounce the Nazis as Bolsheviks — without effect. Despite hostility and indifference from the organized industrial *Arbeiterschaft*, the party's appeal found considerable resonance among that sizable body of workers in handicrafts and small-scale manufacturing. These workers were usually employed in small shops or in government enterprises and were rarely integrated into either the organized working class or the entrepreneurial *Mittelstand*. Their support was loudly trumpeted in the Nazi press and was extremely important in establishing the public image the Nazis sought to project, allowing them to maintain, with some degree of credibility, that they had succeeded in bridging the great social divide of German electoral politics.

The generational and sexual composition of the Nazi constituency was also broader than traditionally assumed. Usually treated as the party of youth, the NSDAP, in fact, found its greatest electoral support among groups composed of older voters. The party effectively pursued the vote of the *Rentnermittelstand*, 53 percent of whom were over sixty years of age. Similarly, less than 10 percent of the shopkeepers, self-employed artisans, and other entrepreneurs in the old middle class were under thirty. In addition, the male-dominated NSDAP attracted a steadily increasing percentage of women voters after 1928. In the final elections of the Weimar era, women appear to have surpassed men in the Nazi electorate.

By 1932 the NSDAP could, therefore, approach the German electorate claiming the coveted mantle of a *Volkspartei*. Its constituency was certainly broader than that of the traditional bourgeois parties or of the Marxist left. Yet, even after the NSDAP's dramatic surge between 1929 and 1932, the limits of its expansion were clearly defined by the two most prominent predictors of German electoral behavior, class and religion. Although the Nazis had won adherents within the blue-collar electorate, they proved unable to establish a significant foothold within the industrial working class. Among workers in the major industrial sectors, electoral sympathies continued to be divided chiefly between the SPD and KPD. Even as unemployment soared after 1928, working-class radicalism found political expression in a Communist vote, not in support for National Socialism. The fragmentation of political loyalties that had increasingly splintered the middle-class electorate after 1924 did not infect the constituencies of the Marxist left. While the liberal, conservative, and special interest parties virtually collapsed between 1930 and 1932, the Marxist parties maintained a remarkably strong and stable electoral base. Despite their efforts to cultivate a working-class constituency, the Nazis were confronted by a solid bloc of blue-collar support for the Marxist left that showed no signs of disintegration even at the apex of Nazi electoral fortunes.

The NSDAP also encountered a major obstacle to its ambitions in the Catholic population. Although the party won an increasing percentage of the Catholic vote after 1928, its electoral base remained far smaller in Catholic Germany than in Protestant areas. Catholic support for National Socialism was by and large concentrated in the same occupational and social groups that formed the mainstays of the party's constituency in Protestant areas, but the NSDAP was never able to undermine the solid foundation of Catholic support for the Zentrum. Backed by the Church, the Zentrum, like the Marxist parties, offered its followers a well-defined belief system vigorously reinforced by an extensive network of political, social, and cultural organizations. Although a vote for the Zentrum after 1930 was hardly an enthusiastic endorsement of the Weimar system, the strong Catholic support for the party continued to impose a solid barrier to the potential expansion of the National Socialist constituency.

Given these limitations to the appeal of National Socialism, what does the composition of the Nazi constituency reveal about the social foundations of fascism in Germany? First, the most consistent electoral support for the party was concentrated in those social and occupational groups that harbored the greatest reservations about the development of modern industrial society and that expressed, through their organizations, socially exclusive, corporatist views of their socioeconomic position. By the same token, its appeal was weakest in that segment of the population most prominently identified with modern industrial society, the industrial working class. Even within the new middle class, where electoral sympathies were scattered across the political spectrum, support for National Socialism was concentrated to a surprising extent in the traditionally conservative civil service. . . .

Nazi antimodernism was, therefore, not a simple assault on modern technology or a promise to dismantle one of the world's most advanced industrial economies and return to a romanticized agrarian past. It was instead a fundamental rejection of the social and political implications of modernization, a rejection that found its most vivid expression in the NSDAP's visceral attacks on both Marxist socialism and liberal capitalism. It was in the party's relentless offensive against these manifestations of modern political and economic life that the NSDAP's anti-Semitism was most prominently displayed before 1933. While Rosenberg and other party theorists continued to develop — and publish — the radical racial doctrine that formed the true core of National Socialist ideology, the party's day-to-day political literature tended to emphasize a more familiar form of social and economic anti-Semitism. This strategy of linking Jews with both "supercapitalism" and bolshevism proved doubly effective for the Nazis. On the one hand, it allowed the NSDAP to exploit an already deeply engrained form of anti-Semitic sentiment in German political culture during a period of protracted economic distress; on the other, it lulled even those parties that took public stands against the NSDAP's obsession with "the Jewish question" into the mistaken assumption that it was merely another ephemeral manifestation of that traditional anti-Semitism which had surfaced periodically in the German party system since 1890. . . .

Yet, even at the height of its popularity at the polls, the NSDAP's position as a people's party was tenuous at best. If the party's support was a mile wide, it was at critical points an inch deep. The NSDAP had managed to build a remarkably diverse constituency, overcoming regional divisions, linking town and country, spanning the social divides, and shrinking the gap between confessions. Yet, the basis of that extraordinary electoral alliance was dissatisfaction, resentment, and fear. As a result, the Nazi constituency, even at the pinnacle of the party's electoral popularity, remained highly unstable. Indeed, the fragmentation of the NSDAP's volatile electorate was already under way in November 1932. Whether the Nazis would have been able to maintain their appeal under improving economic conditions remains, of course, a moot question, but for a party of protest such continued success is doubtful. Even in the flush of their victories in 1932, Nazi leaders were aware of the party's vulnerability. "Something has to happen now," Goebbels noted in his diary following the NSDAP's victory in Prussia during April. "We have to come to power in the near future or we will win ourselves to death in these elections." It therefore remains one of history's most tragic ironies that at precisely the moment when the party's electoral support had begun to falter, Hitler was installed as

The Voice of Authority. Propaganda chief Joseph Goebbels preached the Nazi gospel and many believed. His clear diction and ironic wit made Goebbels an effective advocate of his cause. (UPI/Bettmann Newsphotos)

chancellor by representatives of those traditional elites who had done so much to undermine the parliamentary system in Germany and who still believed that the National Socialist movement could be safely harnessed for their reactionary objectives.

A. J. Nicholls

The Final Step to Power

Hitler was determined to receive the Chancellorship and wreak his vengeance on the "Marxists." President Hindenburg, on the other hand, set his face against both Hitler and a cabinet based on parliament. If the Nazis entered the Government it would be as subordinates in a presidential régime. During these months Hitler showed great political courage in refusing anything but the highest post. There were important men in his party, the most prominent being Gregor Strasser, who felt that the Nazi wave had reached its crest and that the time had come to taste the fruits of office. There was reason in this. Hitler's intransigence was beginning to alarm some of his wealthy business patrons. They found von Papen, who was sympathetic to industrial interests, more attractive than earlier Chancellors, and they detected ominous signs of social radicalism in the SA. Some of them cut their links with the Nazis and others became less generous. In the party as a whole the frenzied activism of the previous months could not be maintained without tangible achievements.

The danger to the Nazis was demonstrated in the autumn of 1932 when von Papen, faced with a completely uncooperative Reichstag, dissolved it yet again. On 6 November Germans trooped to the polls once more. Electoral participation was still high, although not the astonishing 83 per cent registered in July. For the first time since 1928 the Nazis lost votes in a Reichstag election, their share of the poll falling from 37.4 per cent to 33.1 per cent. The German Nationalists, who had begun to stress their difference with the Nazis, gained nearly 800,000

From *Weimar and the Rise of Hitler*, by A. J. Nicholls, 1979. Copyright © 1979. Reprinted by permission of St. Martin's Press.

votes, and the People's Party improved its position slightly, though it only returned eleven deputies. Von Papen could claim that he was making ground, despite the fact that his supporters were still a tiny minority. He and President Hindenburg were quite prepared to go on governing without parliament — a breach of the constitution — until they were ready to implement a complete programme of constitutional reform. Von Papen had drawn up a number of public-works schemes which he hoped would ease the unemployment situation. If the army and the President kept their trust in him he might survive.

It was here that von Papen's political inexperience revealed itself. His unpopularity was so widespread that even his colleagues feared a civil war if the government openly violated the constitution on his behalf. Such fears had been increased at the beginning of November, when Nazis and Communists had collaborated to organise a transport strike in Berlin. Acts of sabotage and violence accompanied this extremist alliance. Upbraided by his wealthier sympathisers, Hitler replied that, unless he allowed his rank and file to take such action, they would desert to the Communists. Reichswehr commanders were alarmed lest their soldiers should have to fight the SA and the Communists. They thought the Poles might take the opportunity to attack Germany. Their anxiety was almost certainly exaggerated. A partnership between Nazis and Communists would have been difficult to maintain and would have aroused fierce opposition from such disparate political elements as the Reichsbanner and the Stahlhelm. Nevertheless, von Schleicher, now convinced that von Papen was a liability, stressed the dark side of the military picture, and his cabinet colleagues agreed with him. Von Papen resigned.

On 2 December von Schleicher himself became Chancellor. It was an exposed position which he had not coveted. Power without responsibility had been his goal. In one important respect he was even weaker than von Papen. His relations with the President had grown cooler since the previous spring. Von Papen had quite replaced him in Hindenburg's favour.

Von Schleicher was an ingenious man who did not lack courage. Having failed once more to negotiate with Hitler, he attempted to create popular support for his government by cutting across normal party lines. Gregor Strasser, still regarded as Hitler's main rival within the Nazi Party, had previously indicated that he might be willing to break with his chief and take office under another Chancellor. Von Schleicher also tried to appeal to the trade unions with schemes of work creation. He envisaged projects for compulsory youth training and cheap labour for farmers. Had he remained in office, he was even prepared to consider nationalising the coal and steel industry.

Imaginative though these ideas were, they quickly collapsed in practice. Strasser was forced to resign his offices in the Nazi Party on 8 December. The Christian and Social Democratic Trade Unions rebuffed von Schleicher. In desperation he turned to the Social Democrats but, fortified with the belief that the Nazi tide had turned, they refused to join his government. Schleicher was forced to ask Hindenburg for the power to govern unconstitutionally — something which had been refused to von Papen.

The President had no desire to accept this. Besides, it was not necessary. Von Papen had been negotiating with Hitler, and had convinced Hindenburg that the Nazi leader should be given the post of Chancellor. Von Papen was confident he could control Hitler. Schleicher had to resign. He greatly feared that Papen would be his successor. The Reichswehr leaders thought that this really would lead to a civil war in which 90 per cent of the nation would be against them. Their apprehension soon disappeared. On 30 January Hitler became Reich Chancellor.

His appointment was quite unnecessary. His coalition government, in which Hugenberg's Nationalists were the only other party represented, had no majority in the Reichstag. The Nazis could not have threatened the State if they had been denied power. Their movement was waning. A further period of frustration might have finished them off. It was perhaps for this reason that Hitler became attractive to men of property in Germany. If his mass support ebbed away the beneficiaries would either be the democratic Weimar parties or the Communists. The dream of national resurgence based on an authoritarian régime would then have been destroyed.

In any case, von Papen and his friends thought they could manage the Nazis. Hitler's men had only two major posts in the Reich government, those of the Chancellor and Minister of the Interior. Von Papen was Vice-Chancellor and Prime Minister of Prussia, and had the ear of the President. A general, Blomberg, headed the Defence Ministry. Hugenberg was Minister of Economics and Food, and Seldte, the Stahlhelm leader, Minister of Labour. There seemed little danger that the Nazis would overwhelm their colleagues.

Within a month Hitler had demonstrated how complacent von Papen had been. Having made a show of negotiating for a coalition with the Centre, Hitler persuaded his colleagues to dissolve the Reichstag for a third general election. He promised them that he would not change the complexion of his cabinet even if he won. The election campaign was conducted under quite unfair conditions, because the authority of the state was at Hitler's disposal. Göring had been appointed Prussian Minister of the Interior, and thus controlled police power in almost two-thirds of Germany. He recruited 50,000 "auxiliary police," most of whom were Nazi storm-troopers. The regular police were purged and ordered to protect Nazis and Nationalists against "Marxist" attack.

On 27 February the Reichstag in Berlin was set on fire by a young Dutchman of extreme left-wing opinions. Using this as a pretext to claim that Germany was threatened by a Bolshevik *coup*, Hitler issued a presidential decree "for the Protection of the People and the State." For many years this was to be one of the main foundations of Nazi tyranny. It swept away constitutional safeguards against arbitrary arrest and the suppression of free speech. A wave of arrests followed. Hitler's opponents believed that the Reichstag fire had been a Nazi plot. This now seems unlikely, but the issue is not an important one. The Nazis had made preparations to take emergency action before the fire, and, had it not occurred, other excuses would have been found.

The Reichstag elections on 5 April did not give Hitler an absolute majority, despite the enormous pressure exerted on the electorate. But with almost 44 per cent of the vote, and in coalition with Hugenberg's Nationalists, Hitler could command a simple majority in the Reichstag. The opposition to him was completely incapable of offering effective resistance. The Centre Party had already shown itself willing to collaborate with Hitler, and its leader, prelate Kaas, now desired only to safeguard the religious freedom of German Catholics. The parties of the moderate right had already been destroyed as an electoral force in the summer of 1932. The Communists were arrested or forced into hiding. Only the Social Democrats tried to put a brave face on defeat. When, on 23 March 1933, Hitler presented the Reichstag with an enabling law empowering him to rule by decree, the Social Democrats were the one group to vote against it. With that last gesture of defiance, their Weimar Republic was finally interred. Hitler was the master of Germany.

The Master Demagogue. By combining the strengths (and flaws) of his natural personality with artfully contrived gestures, Hitler fashioned a charismatic presence that enabled him to achieve absolute power over an entire nation. (Wide World Photos)

PART

II The Personality of the Leader

Variety of Opinion

> It is pointless to speculate about possible breakdowns suffered during his adolescence, Oedipal complexes, unrequited love, etc.
>
> Karl Deitrich Bracher

> So much has been made of the charismatic nature of Hitler's leadership that it is easy to forget the astute and cynical politician in him. It is this mixture of calculation and fanaticism, with the difficulty of telling where one ends and the other begins, which is the peculiar characteristic of Hitler's personality: to ignore or underestimate either is to present a distorted picture.
>
> Alan Bullock

> Hitler was different. In his case certain dominant traits came to the fore which, although they cannot immediately be dubbed "abnormal," did approach the abnormal and are best described in psychopathological terms.
>
> Ernst Nolte

> Aided by the insights of psychoanalysis, let us set forth here our best guesses as to the causes of Hitler's feelings of guilt. One possibility can quickly be eliminated. Hitler felt no remorse whatever over the calculated murder of millions.
>
> Robert G. L. Waite

> *When the subject of study is a modern totalitarian mass movement it requires analysis utilizing all the tools for perceiving and conceptualizing irrational and affective behavior that the twentieth century has to offer, including psychoanalysis and dynamic psychology.*
>
> Peter Loewenberg

Scarcely a publication appeared in Germany after 1933 that did not contain a flattering portrait of Adolf Hitler; and none failed to praise his qualities of leadership. He was above and beyond all else the Führer *of his nation. What was there, then, about this man which found such resonance in the German people? The problem of the "great man" and his times is, of course, one of the old chestnuts of history. But in this instance it need not be considered in abstraction, since we now have access to some of the most intimate details of Hitler's private and public life.*

Karl Dietrich Bracher *strips away the layers of myth that surround Hitler's youth and soberly exposes the more banal reality. He takes careful account of the research of other scholars, but he refuses to elaborate far beyond what has actually been documented. This is a comparison of fantasy and fact rather than a psychological probing. Yet Bracher acknowledges the psychopathic nature of Hitler's world view* (Weltanschauung), *and he attempts to delineate the sources of Hitler's racism and fanatic German nationalism.*

Alan Bullock *portrays the more mature Hitler and the baffling paradoxes of his character: self-deception and shrewd calculation, passion and intuition, cynicism and a sense of mission. In these ambiguities, Bullock believes, lay the secret of Hitler's immense personal charm and his unusual flair for propaganda. Here we can see the dictator at his best and at his worst, and we can recognize those qualities that made him both attractive and repulsive.*

Ernst Nolte *does not hesitate to expand on three traits of Hitler's personality — infantilism, monomania, and mediumism — which distinguished him from the other fascist leaders of Europe. Yet Nolte, too, stops short of claiming that a clinical analysis of Hitler's character is feasible or that, even so, this would suffice to explain the man and the magnetism he exercised on the masses who acclaimed him as their leader.*

Robert G. L. Waite *has ventured into the literature of psychobiography in order to fathom Hitler's emotional life. He concludes that the* Führer *was a man driven by feelings of guilt and inferiority, by fears about the "impurity" of his own blood and his warped sexuality. Hence Hitler's morbid concern with the possibility of defeat, the constant preoccupation with suicide and death, the predilection for religious imagery, and the rabid antipathy for all things Jewish. Waite remains perfectly aware of the speculative nature of psychoanalysis, yet he believes the serious student must confront these matters squarely rather than leave them to salacious gossip.*

Peter Loewenberg *exemplifies a psychohistorical approach to the subject. By drawing on a variety of comparative, literary, and quantitative sources, he joins Waite in departing from the canons of conventional explanation. But he differs in drawing attention away from Hitler's unique personality, emphasizing instead the psychological profile of those who responded to him. Loewenberg sees the key to understanding the generation of the "Nazi youth cohort" in their common experience of material, nutritional, and familial deprivation during the First World War. This technique of inquiry may be easily caricatured — as if Nazism were the result of a decline in breast-feeding — but it is one that deserves careful consideration as a means of grasping the enthusiasm of the masses stirred by Hitler's oratory.*

These selections leave no doubt as to the indispensability of Hitler to the Nazi movement. But they leave in question the adequacy of traditional biography to comprehend such a complex and devious personality. And, if it is inadequate, should we regard psychobiography and psychohistory as complementary or contradictory methods of analysis? The more stress is placed on the importance and idiosyncracy of one man, it would seem, the less compelling are causal explanations of generational conflict within the German population.

Karl Dietrich Bracher

Fantasy and Fact

The triumph of National Socialism over the Weimar Republic and its realization in the Third Reich are so closely connected with the life of

From *The German Dictatorship*, Third Edition, by Karl Dietrich Bracher. Copyright © 1970 by Praeger Publishers, Inc., New York. Reprinted by permission of Praeger Publishers, Inc. and George Weidenfeld and Nicolson Ltd.

Adolf Hitler that one tends to equate the two. National Socialism has also been called "Hitlerism" and "nothing other than the projection of the will of the man Adolf Hitler into the realm of ideas and words," coming into existence with Hitler and also disappearing with him. And the rise, triumph, and defeat of National Socialism undoubtedly cannot be divorced from Hitler. But National Socialism is more than the gigantic mistake of misguided followers, the product solely of the demonic powers of one individual. Some of the intellectual and political currents which fed National Socialism and made possible the emergence of a man like Hitler have already been mentioned. His life must be seen against the background of fin de siècle Austria, and his political rise falls within the framework of postwar Germany and Europe, burdened by grave intellectual and social problems.

Neither Hitler himself nor his closest collaborators, such as National Socialism's chief ideologist, Alfred Rosenberg, or the guiding spirit of Jewish extermination, Reinhard Heydrich, measured up to the prerequisites of the biological postulates of National Socialism: race and ancestry. Official data about Hitler were confined to scant information about his date of birth, scarcely detailed enough for that "small Aryan pass" which he later demanded of all his subjects. Whatever facts about his background have been unearthed give the lie to his story of the harsh early life of an ambitious genius frustrated by circumstances. Still more interesting are the many questions that remain unanswered, beginning with the name and ancestry of the Austrian customs official Alois Hitler; Adolf Hitler, the fourth child of Alois's third marriage, was born on April 20, 1889, in the border town of Braunau am Inn. The name "Hitler" is possibly of Czech origin; the family originally came from the Waldviertel, an Austrian border region near Bohemia. But even this much is not certain, for Alois Hitler, the illegitimate son of a servant girl by the name of Maria Anna Schicklgruber, did not change his name to Hitler until 1876, when he was forty. The identity of Alois's father is not known; Maria Schicklgruber presumably had brought the child with her from the city where she had worked, and, five years after her return, at the age of forty-seven, had married a miller's helper by the name of Georg Hiedler. Almost thirty years after her and Hiedler's deaths, Alois Schicklgruber, with the help of a stepuncle and a gullible village priest, had his birth "legitimized," a step he believed essential to his career and one his stepuncle thought he owed his ambitious ward.

Thus, neither Adolf nor Alois could rightfully claim the name of

Hitler. Later rumors and speculations, reaching the top echelons of National Socialism, thought it highly probable that Hitler had a Jewish grandfather and ascribed the radicalization of anti-Semitism to Hitler's pathological eagerness to repress this fact. However, no conclusive evidence has thus far been turned up. Recent findings indicate that the name of Grandmother Schicklgruber's last employer in Graz was Frankenberger — by no means invariably a Jewish name — and his son might possibly have fathered her child.

Such digressions are as sensational as they are questionable and pointless, for, though well meaning, they are rooted in racist superstitions. Hitler's early years and development, particularly his Vienna period, offer ample explanation for his intellectual and psychological development. He grew up in the secure household of a minor civil servant, by no means as impoverished a home as later legend had it. The nice house of his birth, the family property, and his father's pension would indicate that Hitler's years of poverty were the result of his own failure. The father, contrary to his son's later claims, was not a chronic alcoholic, but, rather, a comparatively progressive man with a good job; the mother devoted herself to the care of their home and children. The only thing that seemed to be lacking was a sensible education. The note of self-pity struck by Hitler in making the sad fate of his early years responsible for his failures, culminating in the moving story of the young orphan who finally had to leave home to earn his living, is as contrived as it is untrue.

In 1892, the family moved from Braunau to Passau (Bavaria) and in 1894, to Linz (Austria). Alois Hitler retired a year later, and for a while ran a farm in the Traun valley; in 1898, he purchased a house in Leonding near Linz. Thus, the symbolic significance which Hitler in *Mein Kampf* ascribed to his being born in Braunau, where in 1812 a patriotic bookdealer by the name of Palm was executed for anti-Napoleonic activities, also has little foundation, for Hitler spent part of his formative years in the Bavarian border town of Passau and the rest in Linz, the capital city of Upper Austria. His school career in Linz (he had to repeat his fifth year and was transferred to another school in his ninth) was a fiasco; Hitler was not only labeled indolent, but his performance in mathematics and shorthand as well as in German was considered unsatisfactory — a judgment borne out by his later style. Contrary to his claims in *Mein Kampf*, his grades in geography and history were only passing; his only above-average marks were in drawing and gymnastics. One of his teachers called him lopsidedly talented, uncontrolled, high-handed, dogmatic, ill-tempered, lacking in perseverance, and despotic.

After the death of his father (1903), his mother afforded the highschool dropout two-and-a-half years of idleness (1905–1907), which he spent daydreaming, occasionally drawing, and going to the theater. At this time, the sixteen-year-old began to manifest some of the traits that marked the later political fanatic and demagogue: utter self-involvement to the point of hysterical self-pity, a mania for untrammeled speechifying and equally grandiose and uncontrolled plan making, combined with listlessness and an inability to concentrate, let alone work productively. The serious lung disease which Hitler invoked to explain the way he lived is pure invention. A sentence in *Mein Kampf* about the end of his school career is most revealing: "Suddenly I was helped by an illness." The life he led after failing at school was exactly the sort of life that appealed to him. The irresponsible lack of restraint of his Vienna years may be seen as a direct consequence of his two years of idleness. It is simply not true that financial need was responsible for his life in Vienna. Even after the death of his overindulgent mother in late 1907, Adolf and his sister, Paula, were financially secure.

The Hitler myth has it that the seventeen-year-old, forced to earn his living, had to go to that decadent metropolis, Vienna. The fact is that in 1906, his mother treated him to a trip to Vienna, where he passed the time sightseeing and going to the theater, particularly to his beloved Wagner operas. The next year was spent in the protected setting of his mother's house. Neither school nor work was allowed to interrupt his routine. The only "work" he did was occasional drawings, and his grandiose plans for the rebuilding of Linz foreshadowed the extravagant ideas of the master builder of the Third Reich. These youthful fantasies reemerged in the "monumental" designs he prepared after his entry into Linz in 1938. The pre-Vienna period of this "work-shy dreamer" already contained the seeds of the type of life and thoughts which have come to light in studies of Hitler's early years. An episode of 1906 is typical: he had an idea for a large-scale research project, complete with housekeeper and cook, which was to afford him and his musician friend August Kubizek the necessary leisure and comfort for the study of "German art" and the formation of a circle of "art lovers," said project to be realized through the purchase of a winning lottery ticket. According to his friend, "Adolf Hitler could plan and look into the future so beautifully that I could have listened to him forever." Equally typical is the violence with which he reacted to the news that he had won neither the first nor any of the other lottery prizes: it was the fault of the "entire social order." This episode offers an almost uncanny preview of the later Hitler.

It is pointless to speculate about possible breakdowns suffered during his adolescence, Oedipal complexes, unrequited love, etc. Understandably enough, the relatives of the young man of leisure who refused to entertain any idea about simply "working for a living" began to pressure him to learn a trade. Having failed in his efforts to gain admission to the Vienna Academy of Art (September 1907), he gave no thought to the possibility of any other profession. He stayed on in Vienna, living the comfortable life of the "art student," without telling his ailing mother the truth. After his mother's death, he still was not under any immediate financial pressure; there was a substantial inheritance in addition to his orphan's allowance, which he continued to collect until his twenty-third year under the pretext of being enrolled at the Vienna Academy. Later, he also inherited a fairly substantial sum from an aunt. All these facts underscore the dishonesty of the piteous note struck in his autobiography.

The nineteen-year-old Hitler floundering in Vienna did not, contrary to the self-image of *Mein Kampf*, have any definite political orientation. His "nationalism" was in line with the national German tendencies prevalent in Linz, and his knowledge of history, in which he allegedly excelled at school, was limited. As late as the 1930s, his history instructor, Leopold Pötsch, of whom he speaks highly in *Mein Kampf*, did not want to be part of this myth. As to the "Jewish problem," Hitler also had little knowledge and no firm opinions. His family doctor was Jewish, and Hitler used to send him hand-painted postcards from Vienna. He also accepted money gifts from him, yet in 1938, after the Anschluss, the doctor was driven into exile. Against these facts we have Hitler's contention that while in Linz he had already learned "to understand and comprehend the meaning of history" and that the Austrian nationality conflict had taught him that the meaning of history was to be found in the battle for the "nation" (*Volkstum*) and in the victory of "völkisch nationalism" (*Mein Kampf*, pp. 8 ff.). Yet, some of the basic traits and thoughts which took shape during his five-and-a-half years in Vienna were, according to Kubizek, his patient audience, already to be found in the endless speeches and grandiose plans of his

Linzer days. The experiences of Vienna, Munich, and World War I lent them substance and embellished them with the up-to-date content and impulses which so profoundly were to shape Hitler the political man.

He was driven to Vienna not by "need and harsh reality" but by the desire to escape work, the need to learn a trade, and the wish to continue the life-style of the "future artist," a pose which he was unable to maintain any longer under the watchful eyes of his relatives in Linz. He kept on urging his friend Kubizek to join him in Vienna. In the ensuing months, he was an almost daily visitor to the opera, went sightseeing, developed grandiose plans for a musical drama and for all sorts of building projects, while Kubizek, who had been as unaware of his friend's academic failure as the family, enrolled in the Vienna Conservatory. Hitler, as he proudly stated, was supreme master of his time. The harsh life of the "common laborer" who had to earn his "crust of bread" is one of the heart-rending myths of his autobiography. Between 1909 and 1913, the unsuccessful art student and self-designated "artist" and "writer" was introduced to the political ideas and currents that were to furnish the decisive concepts and stimuli for his later career. The political and social conflicts and emotions in the Vienna of that era offered material and food for a radical critique of society, and the unbridgeable gap between Hitler's wants, ambitions, and fantasies and naked reality made him accept and enlarge on this critique. It was the same impulse that later, in crisis-ridden postwar Germany, drove so large a segment of the lower middle class, its feelings of superiority threatened, into the arms of the radical-Right doctrine of salvation — a sociopolitical flight into an irrational political creed thriving on hatred and fear and demanding to be saved from conflict through the institution of a total "new order."

The rejection of Hitler's second application for admission to the Art Academy in the fall of 1908 seems to have been a turning point in his life. He broke off his friendship with Kubizek and became submerged in the shadowy world of public shelters (1908–1909) and homes for men (1910–1913), though the allowance and the gifts from relatives continued. Moreover, the "hard labor" referred to in *Mein Kampf* should have brought him additional funds. During this period, Hitler discovered the political and social slogans then in vogue, an encounter reminiscent of his earlier introduction to art. Contrary to his testimony, Hitler had read few books and had not really concerned himself with the political and social problems of his environment. A chance reading of books, occasional pamphlets, and generalizations based on subjective impressions combined to form the distorted political picture which, in almost pristine form, became the "weltanschauung" that dominated Hitler's future life and work.

The only work he did was an occasional copying of picture postcards which his fellow inmates of the men's home sold for him. He spent most of his time piecing together his weltanschauung from obscure sources. Its essence was extreme nationalism and a radical racial anti-Semitism. The literature which stimulated Hitler's interest in politics forms the subject of a comprehensive study. Among his reading matter was a periodical with the resounding name of *Ostara*, the German goddess of spring, a publication which, from 1905 on, was widely sold in the tobacco kiosks of Vienna. It gave voice to the eccentric and bloodthirsty race mythology of Adolf Lanz (1874–1954), an ex-monk who called himself Lanz von Liebenfels. His program called for the founding of a male order of blue-eyed, blond "Aryans." His headquarters were in a castle in Lower Austria which he had bought with the help of industrialist patrons. There Lanz hoisted the swastika banner in 1906 as the symbol of the Aryan movement. This pathological founding father of an "Aryan" hero cult was the author of *Theozoology* (1901), a work offering a particularly abstruse mixture of an extreme, pseudoreligious racism. Apparently, Hitler got in touch with Lanz personally in 1909, asking for copies of *Ostara* that were missing from his own collection. Lanz's views, and similarly fantastic notions from the "European underground," which later were to make their way into the Ludendorff movement, helped to shape Hitler's political ideology. Lanz's works disseminated the crass exaggerations of the Social Darwinist theory of survival, the superman and superrace theory, the dogma of race conflict, and the breeding and extermination theories of the future SS state. The scheme was simple: a blond, heroic race of "Arioheroes" was engaged in battle with inferior mixed races whose annihilation was deemed a historico-political necessity; "race defilement" was not to be tolerated, and the master race was to multiply with the help of "race hygiene," polygamy, and breeding stations; sterilization, debilitating forced labor, and systematic liquidation were to offer a final solution.

Such pamphlets were fatal reading for an unstable youth with few ideas of his own, even though, as Hitler himself confessed, his middleclass, liberal background initially led him to rebel against these teach-

The Young Hitler. Even as an aspiring politician, Hitler in 1921 already possessed the riveting gaze that projected his steely determination to achieve national prominence and power. (© Topham/The Image Works)

ings. This literature took on great significance against the background of impressions received by a footloose youth on the lowest rung of the social ladder in the capital city of a multinational monarchy. Hitler's acquaintance with Marxist socialism also was not the product of close study, as he claimed, but of obscure subjective impressions marked by the sort of class and cultural snobbery which was still part of him and which he now directed toward social and political issues. A passage in *Mein Kampf* (p. 25), precisely because of its exaggeration, throws interesting light on its author and the substance of his weltanschauung: "At that time I read ceaselessly and very thoroughly." (He never is specific about his reading matter; his "books," according to his own account of the genesis of his anti-Semitism [p. 59], are polemical pamphlets bought "for a few pennies.") The passage continues: "What free time I had left from my work was spent on my studies. In a few years I thus created for myself the basis of the knowledge on which I still feed. During that time I formed a picture of the world and an ideology which has become the granite foundation of my deeds. I only had to add a little more knowledge to that which I had acquired at that time; I did not have to revise anything."

Who else can say this of his impressions at the age of twenty? This passage is more revealing of the level of his Viennese "studies" (mostly, endless debates between the idle smart aleck and his fellow inmates at the shelter) and of the substance of the later National Socialist ideology than the most probing analysis. What Hitler "learned" in Vienna, and subsequently elevated to the status of a "constructive ideology," was that monomaniacal, obsessive, unseeing yet effective method of political argumentation which led from the evenings in the men's shelter of Vienna to the endless monologues of the demagogue.

In addition to inventing the story of the day laborer who while on the job had his eyes opened to Marxism and its Jewish "backers." Hitler also makes mention of the anti-Semitic movement of the Austro-Pan-German nationalist von Schönerer. The actual impact of this anti-monarchist, anti-Marxist social movement, the Austrian version of a decidedly national "German socialism," is hard to assess, but its nationalist, völkisch battle cries undoubtedly are among the roots of National Socialism. They furnished the young Hitler with a political framework for his personal and social resentments against a society in which his adolescent daydreams and wants found neither response nor expression.

The substance of the ideas which Hitler made into the "granite foundation" of his future policies has been paraphrased repeatedly. It is nothing more than a sweeping rejection of and opposition to tolerance and cosmopolitanism, democracy and parliamentarianism, Marxism and Jewry, which, in primitive equation, were called the primary evils of the world. Even then, however, the core, probably the only "genuine" fanatically held and realized conviction of his entire life, was anti-Semitism and race mania. An enormously oversimplified scheme of good and evil, transplanted to the biological and racial sphere, was made to serve as the master key to the history of political thought. Hitler's fanatical hatred of the Jews defies all rational explanation; it cannot be measured by political and pragmatic gauges. The fact that an entire nation followed him and furnished a legion of executioners does demonstrate, however, that we are confronted not merely with the inexplicable dynamics of one man, but with a terrible disease of modern nationalism, whose desire for exclusivity and war against everything "alien" constitutes one of the root causes of anti-Semitism.

The psychopathic features of Hitler's weltanschauung were discernible even then: the social envy of the failure and the discrepancy between his exalted vision of personal prestige and the poverty of the unemployed man who held ordinary work in disdain both played a role. The much-abused Nietzsche once called anti-Semitism the ideology of the "those who feel cheated." Unconfirmed rumor has it that Hitler arrived at the "awareness" that the creative person — and he, being a painter, belonged to this category — gets cheated by the sly, worldly, aggressive Jewish trader after he himself had had an unpleasant experience with a Jewish art dealer. Such personal resentments may have contributed to the rationalization of his perverse anti-Semitism.

At about that time, Hitler had also become a "fanatical nationalist." At its highest pitch, nationalist ideology appeals to mass insanity, assuming the force of a collective psychosis in which the annihilation of the enemy spells one's own success and salvation. The anti-Semitic atmosphere of the Vienna of that time provided Hitler's new eclectic philosophy with the firm base on which militant nationalism could develop to its most extreme form and be carried to the point of absurdity. The Jews are the cause of all misfortune; ruthless battle against them holds the key to national if not universal salvation: this precept formed the base of Hitler's later nationalism and imperialism, which ultimately combined forcible expansion beyond the national boundaries with the missionary zeal of a German war on "world Jewry." After Hitler became chancellor, he confided to intimates that he had been compelled to resort to nationalism because of "the conditions of the times," but that he had always been convinced that "we have to get rid of this false conception" of democracy and liberalism and in its place "set up . . . the conception of race, which has not yet been politically used up."

The "studies" and "harsh lessons" of his Vienna years, which Hitler said were the foundation of his entire career, thus provided the immature youth with the kind of banal, limited semieducation which is among the most dangerous impulses for the destructive forces of our time. Just as he failed to persevere in school and work, this rambling autodidact failed to gain real insight into the problems of the time. His tirelessly fundamental, global "debates" with Marxism and democracy, despite their manic repetition, also never went beyond generalities and platitudes. In *Mein Kampf*, he describes the method of reading and studying through which he acquired his pseudoeducation: he always knew how to separate the wheat from the chaff and to extract the true content of everything. In this way, he gathered a store of semi-information which he put to good use; his was a "pigeonhole mind" (*Heiber*), lacking the ability to see things in their context. But, at the same time, he satisfied his adolescent "striving for self-worth" (*Daim*) and also developed a set of ideas of whose simplicity he was to furnish proof. When, in 1924, Hitler proudly told a Munich court that by the time he left Vienna he had become "an absolute anti-Semite, a mortal enemy of the entire Marxist philosophy, Pan-German in my political convictions," he was probably telling the truth (*Mein Kampf*, pp. 130 ff.).

In May 1913, a year later than stated in *Mein Kampf*, Hitler suddenly turned up in Munich, after more than five years of obscurity. The reasons for his abrupt departure from Vienna are not clear. One might think he was telling the truth when he said that he was prompted by a dislike for the Habsburg Empire and a yearning for the Bavarian art capital, were it not for the recent revelation of an embarrassing episode. It seems that this future ideologist of combat, the "military genius," had evaded military service in 1909–1910, just as he had evaded all other duties, quite unlike those reviled "homeless" Marxists and Jews. Like all of Hitler's major "decisions" — leaving school, moving to Vienna, going to war, entering politics, again going to war, and, finally, his egocentric fall — the road to Munich was also an escape route, this time from military service. This is attested to also by the fact that the then twenty-four-year-old Hitler, who, in fact, remained a citizen of Austria until 1925, called himself "stateless." When arrested and extradited to Salzburg at the request of Austria, he fawningly told the court about his sad life, and, in fact, his poor physical condition saved him from punishment and conscription. Hitler's long letter of explanation (January 1914) to the Linz authorities hints at the legend of later years. When he writes, "I have never known the lovely word 'youth,'" it almost reads like a "draft for *Mein Kampf*" (Jetzinger). This shameful affair, the documents of which became the object of a feverish search after Hitler's invasion of Austria, testifies to his dishonesty and cowardice and to the mendacity of a weltanschauung whose rigorous precepts were valid only for others.

He fared no better in Munich than he had in Vienna. The sale of his bad paintings brought in little. The future looked no rosier in Germany. The outbreak of World War I almost seemed like salvation. A rare photograph of that time shows Hitler, wearing a dashing artist's hat, among the masses at the Odeonsplatz cheering the news that war had been declared. Carried away by the popular enthusiasm, he felt liberated from his unproductive, unsuccessful life. As a volunteer not expected to act or decide independently, freed from the purposeless existence of the occasional painter and coffeehouse habitué incapable of establishing personal relationships, he now found himself subject to a discipline which, unlike the disreputable camaraderie of the Vienna shelter, also satisfied his dreams of national and social grandeur. Hitler later justified and glorified the fact that he served in the German army rather than that of his homeland by denouncing the Habsburg Empire, however inconsistent this may have seemed with his critical attitude toward Wilhelmian Germany. The fact that once more he found himself in a male community indelibly affected his future life and ideas. "Destiny," which he liked to invoke, had pointed the way: "To me, those times were like a deliverance from the vexing emotions of my youth . . . so that, overcome by passionate enthusiasm, I fell to my knees and thanked heaven out of an overflowing heart" (*Mein Kampf*, p. 177). The war seemed to put an end to all problems of daily life in a society in which he had not been able to find his way and which, in typically egocentric fashion, he held responsible for his failure. This, not the dramatically stilted phrase of 1918 ("I, however, decided to become a politician"), was the decisive turning point; war as the transmutation of all values, battle as the father of all things, was the dominant force of Hitler's future life. Hence the eagerly sought-for prolongation of the war beyond the peace agreement into the crises and civil-war atmosphere of the Weimar Republic became the basis of Hitler's activities.

Little worth mentioning happened to Hitler during the war years. Though as a courier he remained a mere corporal, he did have occasion to distinguish himself. He remained a loner, nonsmoker, teetotaler, and lover of sweets, a model patriot and tireless polemicist against Jews, Marxists, and defeatists; he had little in common with the ordinary soldier. The pronounced ascetic-heroic "idealism," the bent toward the undeviatingly radical, the rejection of "ordinary" and erotic pleasures, the feeling of superiority and the sacrificing of personal interests for a "higher ideal" — all these were already hinted at in his monologues and schemes in Linz. Later, Hitler permitted these tendencies to be magnified into an effective myth of a demigod free from ordinary human needs and failings. This, too, was, in effect, an escape, an "escape into legend" (Heiden).

It was the discipline of war and the "front-line acquaintance" with the clear and simple military hierarchy of order and values which were to shape Hitler's sense of values and turn this unstable dreamer unable to come to terms with the bourgeois world of work and order into the rigid fanatic with incredibly oversimplified ideas of war and order. This military male order was the model for the future armed party organizations, for the ideal of a "national community" ready for battle, and for the leader idea; it was elevated to the guiding principle of the political, social, and intellectual life of the country. Therefore Germany's defeat, news of which reached Hitler in the field hospital of Pasewalk, where he was being treated for gas poisoning, not only touched his patriotic feelings but affected his very existence: he was faced with the prospect of returning to his miserable prewar existence. The war simply could not be over, and if, as Hitler was convinced, it had been lost because of defeatism on the home front and the Jewish-Marxist "stab in the back," then this conviction had to be validated by continuing the fight at home. This "national" necessity took on existential significance for Hitler. Ever since those liberating days of 1914, the private and now "professional" life of Hitler, a man with little education and no personal ties, had been based on perpetuating the state of war. It was this which lay at the root of the fanatical energy with which Hitler turned the war into his motivating principle. That is how he looked at politics as a career — as a means for gaining power which would make possible a new war, this one, however, fought according to his ideas until final victory was won.

Hitler's turn to politics also was not the logical outcome of his own decision and resolution, as the legend of *Mein Kampf* would have it. It, too, was an escape from regular work; once again, having returned to Munich, he let events force a decision on him, one, however, to which he held fast. But, initially, Hitler did little to translate into fact his alleged decision of November 9, 1918, "to get into politics." Fearing civilian life, he clung to the security of military service and witnessed, from his barracks, the brief turmoil of the Munich *Räterepublik* (April 1919). Only later was he given the opportunity, for the first time in his life, to exercise a political function. His "nationalistic" zeal in the service of a commission engaged in ferreting out revolutionary elements among the troops persuaded his superiors to make him an "information officer" responsible for the nationalist education and control of his comrades. Since this assignment involved contact with rightist groups, he found himself, in September 1919, as an observer at a meeting of one of the numerous new small right-wing parties, the German Workers' Party, in a Munich beer hall.

This chance happening was to make history and decide Hitler's career. Drexler's group of sectarians and beer-hall politicians gathered at this meeting to listen to a speech by the engineer Feder about the abolition of capitalism and the rule of finance capital; the speech was not very impressive. But Hitler felt at home in this uncritical assemblage, and so when informed some time later of his admission into the party, though he himself had never applied, he accepted. He became Party Comrade No. 55, and, simultaneously, the seventh member of the executive committee. Hitler may have been incapable of taking the initiative, let alone of founding a political party, but, once a decision had been made without his active help, he zealously threw himself into the new role of politician. In view of the disarmament provisions of the Versailles treaty, his days in the rump army were probably numbered anyway; now he found the framework which might possibly combine the ideas of his Vienna days with a wartime order, offering him a chance to use his modicum of "learning" to secure his existence and to compensate for his fear of the demands of a civilian life in which he had failed.

Alan Bullock

Deception and Calculation

The foundation of Hitler's success was his own energy and ability as a political leader. Without this, the help would never have been forthcoming, or would have produced insignificant results. Hitler's genius as a politician lay in his unequalled grasp of what could be done by propaganda, and his flair for seeing how to do it. He had to learn in a hard school, on his feet night after night, arguing his case in every kind of hall, from the smoke-filled back room of a beer cellar to the huge auditorium of the Zirkus Krone; often, in the early days, in the face of opposition, indifference, or amused contempt; learning to hold his audience's attention, to win them over; most important of all, learning to read the minds of his audiences, finding the sensitive spots on which to hammer. "He could play like a virtuoso on the well-tempered piano of lower middle-class hearts," says Dr. Schacht. Behind that virtuosity lay years of experience as an agitator and mob orator. Hitler came to know Germany and the German people at first hand as few of Germany's other leaders ever had. By the time he came to power in 1933 there were few towns of any size in the Reich where he had not spoken. Here was one great advantage Hitler had over nearly all the politicians with whom he had to deal, his immense practical experience of politics, not in the Chancellery or the Reichstag, but in the street, the level at which elections are won, the level at which any politician must be effective if he is to carry a mass vote with him.

Hitler was the greatest demagogue in history. Those who add "only

From *Hitler: A Study in Tyranny*, Revised Edition, by Alan Bullock. Copyright © 1962 by Alan Bullock. Reprinted by permission of Harper & Row, Publishers, Inc.

a demagogue" fail to appreciate the nature of political power in an age of mass politics. As he himself said: "To be a leader, means to be able to move masses."

The lessons which Hitler drew from the activities of the Austrian Social Democrats and Lueger's Christian Socialists were now tried out in Munich. Success was far from being automatic. Hitler made mistakes and had much to learn before he could persuade people to take him seriously, even on the small stage of Bavarian politics. By 1923 he was still only a provincial politician, who had not yet made any impact on national politics, and the end of 1923 saw the collapse of his movement in a fiasco. But Hitler learned from his mistakes, and by the time he came to write *Mein Kampf* in the middle of the 1920s he was able to set down quite clearly what he was trying to do, and what were the conditions of success. The pages in *Mein Kampf* in which he discusses the technique of mass propaganda and political leadership stand out in brilliant contrast with the turgid attempts to explain his entirely unoriginal political ideas.

The first and most important principle for political action laid down by Hitler is: Go to the masses. "The movement must avoid everything which may lessen or weaken its power of influencing the masses . . . because of the simple fact that no great idea, no matter how sublime or exalted, can be realized in practice without the effective power which resides in the popular masses."

> *Since the masses have only a poor acquaintance with abstract ideas, their reactions lie more in the domain of the feelings, where the roots of their positive as well as their negative attitudes are implanted. . . . The emotional grounds of their attitude furnish the reason for their extraordinary stability. It is always more difficult to fight against faith than against knowledge. And the driving force which has brought about the most tremendous revolutions on this earth has never been a body of scientific teaching which has gained power over the masses, but always a devotion which has inspired them, and often a kind of hysteria which has urged them into action. Whoever wishes to win over the masses must know the key that will open the door to their hearts. It is not objectivity, which is a feckless attitude, but a determined will, backed up by power where necessary.*

Hitler is quite open in explaining how this is to be achieved. "The receptive powers of the masses are very restricted, and their understanding is feeble. On the other hand, they quickly forget. Such being the case, all effective propaganda must be confined to a few bare necessities and then must be expressed in a few stereotyped formulas." Hitler had nothing but scorn for the intellectuals who are always looking for something new. "Only constant repetition will finally succeed in imprinting an idea on the memory of a crowd." For the same reason it is better to stick to a program even when certain points in it become out of date: "As soon as one point is removed from the sphere of dogmatic certainty, the discussion will not simply result in a new and better formulation, but may easily lead to endless debates and general confusion."

When you lie, tell big lies. This is what the Jews do, working on the principle, "which is quite true in itself, that in the big lie there is always a certain force of credibility; because the broad masses of a nation are always more easily corrupted in the deeper strata of their emotional nature than consciously or voluntarily, and thus in the primitive simplicity of their minds they more readily fall victims to the big lie than the small lie, since they themselves often tell small lies in little matters, but would be ashamed to resort to large-scale falsehoods. It would never come into their heads to fabricate colossal untruths and they would not believe that others could have the impudence to distort the truth so infamously. . . . The grossly impudent lie always leaves traces behind it, even after it has been nailed down."

Above all, never hesitate, never qualify what you say, never concede an inch to the other side, paint all your contrasts in black and white. This is the "very first condition which has to be fulfilled in every kind of propaganda: a systematically one-sided attitude towards every problem that has to be dealt with. . . . When they see an uncompromising onslaught against an adversary, the people have at all times taken this as proof that right is on the side of the active aggressor; but if the aggressor should go only halfway and fail to push home his success . . . the people will look upon this as a sign that he is uncertain of the justice of his own cause."

Vehemence, passion, fanaticism, these are "the great magnetic forces which alone attract the great masses; for these masses always respond to the compelling force which emanates from absolute faith in the ideas put forward, combined with an indomitable zest to fight for and defend them. . . . The doom of a nation can be averted only by a storm of glowing passion; but only those who are passionate themselves can arouse passion in others."

Hitler showed a marked preference for the spoken over the written

word. "The force which ever set in motion the great historical av-
alanches of religious and political movements is the magic power of the
spoken word. The broad masses of a population are more amenable to
the appeal of rhetoric than to any other force." The employment of
verbal violence, the repetition of such words as "smash," "force" "ruthless," "hatred," was deliberate. Hitler's gestures and the emotional character of his speaking, lashing himself up to a pitch of near hysteria in
which he would scream and spit out his resentment, had the same effect
on an audience. Many descriptions have been given of the way in
which he succeeded in communicating passion to his listeners, so that
men groaned or hissed and women sobbed involuntarily, if only to
relieve the tension, caught up in the spell of powerful emotions of
hatred and exaltation, from which all restraint had been removed.

It was to be years yet before Hitler was able to achieve this effect on
the scale of the Berlin Sportpalast audiences of the 1930s, but he had
already begun to develop extraordinary gifts as a speaker. It was in
Munich that he learned to address mass audiences of several thousands.
In *Mein Kampf* he remarks that the orator's relationship with his audience is the secret of his art. "He will always follow the lead of the great
mass in such a way that from the living emotion of his hearers the apt
word which he needs will be suggested to him and in its turn this will go
straight to the hearts of his hearers." A little later he speaks of the
difficulty of overcoming emotional resistance: this cannot be done by
argument, but only by an appeal to the "hidden forces" in an audience,
an appeal that the orator alone can make. . . .

The conversations recorded by Hermann Rauschning for the period
1932–1934, and by the table talk at the Führer's H.Q. for the period 1941–1942, reveal Hitler in another favorite role, that of visionary
and prophet. This was the mood in which Hitler indulged, talking far
into the night, in his house on the Obersalzberg, surrounded by the
remote peaks and silent forests of the Bavarian Alps; or in the Eyrie he
had built six thousand feet up on the Kehlstein, above the Berghof,
approached only by a mountain road blasted through the rock and a lift
guarded by doors of bronze. There he would elaborate his fabulous
schemes for a vast empire embracing the Eurasian Heartland of the
geopoliticians; his plans for breeding a new elite biologically prese-
lected; his design for reducing whole nations to slavery in the founda-

tion of his new empire. Such dreams had fascinated Hitler since he wrote *Mein Kampf*. It was easy in the late 1920s and early 1930s to dismiss them as the product of a disordered and overheated imagination soaked in the political romanticism of Wagner and Houston Stewart Chamberlain. But these were still the themes of Hitler's table talk in 1941–1942 and by then, master of the greater part of Europe and on the eve (as he believed) of conquering Russia and the Ukraine, Hitler had shown that he was capable of translating his fantasies into a terrible reality. The invasion of Russia, the SS extermination squads, the planned elimination of the Jewish race; the treatment of the Poles and Russians, the Slav *Untermenschen* — these, too, were the fruits of Hitler's imagination.

All this combines to create a picture of which the best description is Hitler's own famous sentence: "I go the way that Providence dictates with the assurance of a sleepwalker." The former French ambassador speaks of him as "a man possessed"; Hermann Rauschning writes: "Dostoevsky might well have invented him, with the morbid derangement and the pseudo-creativeness of his hysteria"; one of the defense counsel at the Nuremberg trials, Dr. Dix, quoted a passage from Goethe's *Dichtung und Wahrheit* describing the Demoniac and applied this very aptly to Hitler. With Hitler, indeed, one is uncomfortably aware of never being far from the realm of the irrational.

But this is only half the truth about Hitler, for the baffling problem about this strange figure is to determine the degree to which he was swept along by a genuine belief in his own inspiration and the degree to which he deliberately exploited the irrational side of human nature, both in himself and others, with a shrewd calculation. For it is salutary to recall, before accepting the Hitler Myth at anything like its face value, that it was Hitler who invented the myth, assiduously cultivating and manipulating it for his own ends. So long as he did this he was brilliantly successful; it was when he began to believe in his own magic, and accept the myth of himself as true, that his flair faltered.

So much has been made of the charismatic nature of Hitler's leadership that it is easy to forget the astute and cynical politician in him. It is this mixture of calculation and fanaticism, with the difficulty of telling where one ends and the other begins, which is the peculiar characteristic of Hitler's personality: to ignore or underestimate either element is to present a distorted picture.

The link between the different sides of Hitler's character was his extraordinary capacity for self-dramatization. "This so-called *Wahnsystem*, or capacity for self-delusion," Sir Nevile Henderson, the British ambassador, wrote, "was a regular part of his technique. It helped him both to work up his own passions and to make his people believe anything that he might think good for them." Again and again one is struck by the way in which, having once decided rationally on a course of action, Hitler would whip himself into a passion which enabled him to bear down all opposition, and provided him with the motive power to enforce his will on others. An obvious instance of this is the synthetic fury, which he could assume or discard at will, over the treatment of German minorities abroad. When it was a question of refusing to listen to the bitter complaints of the Germans in the South Tyrol, or of uprooting the German inhabitants of the Baltic States, he sacrificed them to the needs of his Italian and Russian alliances with indifference. So long as good relations with Poland were necessary to his foreign policy he showed little interest in Poland's German minority. But when it suited his purpose to make the "intolerable wrongs" of the Austrian Nazis, or the Germans in Czechoslovakia and Poland, a ground for action against these states, he worked himself into a frenzy of indignation, with the immediate — and calculated — result that London and Paris, in their anxiety for peace, exerted increased pressure on Prague or Warsaw to show restraint and make further concessions to the German demands.

One of Hitler's most habitual devices was to place himself on the defensive, to accuse those who opposed or obstructed him of aggression and malice, and to pass rapidly from a tone of outraged innocence to the full thunders of moral indignation. It was always the other side who were to blame, and in turn he denounced the Communists, the Jews, the Republican government, or the Czechs, the Poles, and the Bolsheviks for their "intolerable" behavior which forced him to take drastic action in self-defense.

Hitler in a rage appeared to lose all control of himself. His face became mottled and swollen with fury, he screamed at the top of his voice, spitting out a stream of abuse, waving his arms wildly and drumming on the table or the wall with his fists. As suddenly as he had begun he would stop, smooth down his hair, straighten his collar and resume a more normal voice.

This skillful and deliberate exploitation of his own temperament extended to other moods than anger. When he wanted to persuade or win someone over he could display great charm. Until the last days of his life he retained an uncanny gift of personal magnetism which defies analysis, but which many who met him have described. This was connected with the curious power of his eyes, which are persistently said to have had some sort of hypnotic quality. Similarly, when he wanted to frighten or shock, he showed himself a master of brutal and threatening language, as in the celebrated interviews with Schuschnigg and President Hacha.

Yet another variation in his roles was the impression of concentrated willpower and intelligence, the leader in complete command of the situation and with a knowledge of the facts which dazzled the generals or ministers summoned to receive his orders. To sustain this part he drew on his remarkable memory, which enabled him to reel off complicated orders of battle, technical specifications, and long lists of names and dates without a moment's hesitation. Hitler cultivated this gift of memory assiduously. The fact that subsequently the details and figures which he cited were often found to contain inaccuracies did not matter: it was the immediate effect at which he aimed. The swiftness of the transition from one mood to another was startling: one moment his eyes would be filled with tears and pleading, the next blazing with fury, or glazed with the faraway look of the visionary.

Hitler, in fact, was a consummate actor, with the actor's and orator's facility for absorbing himself in a role and convincing himself of the truth of what he was saying at the time he said it. In his early years he was often awkward and unconvincing, but with practice the part became second nature to him, and with the immense prestige of success behind him, and the resources of a powerful state at his command, there were few who could resist the impression of the piercing eyes, the Napoleonic pose, and the "historic" personality.

Hitler had the gift of all great politicians for grasping the possibilities of a situation more swiftly than his opponents. He saw, as no other politician did, how to play on the grievances and resentments of the German people, as later he was to play on French and British fear of war and fear of communism. His insistence upon preserving the forms of legality in the struggle for power showed a brilliant understanding of the way to disarm opposition, just as the way in which he undermined the independence of the German army showed his grasp of the weaknesses of the German Officer Corps.

A German word, *Fingerspitzengefühl* ("finger-tip feeling"), which was often applied to Hitler, well describes his sense of opportunity and timing.

> *No matter what you attempt [Hitler told Rauschning on one occasion], if an idea is not yet mature you will not be able to realize it. Then there is only one thing to do: have patience, wait, try again, wait again. In the subconscious, the work goes on. It matures, sometimes it dies. Unless I have the inner, incorruptible conviction: this is the solution, I do nothing. Not even if the whole Party tries to drive me into action.*

Hitler knew how to wait in 1932, when his insistence on holding out until he could secure the chancellorship appeared to court disaster. Foreign policy provides another instance. In 1939 he showed great patience while waiting for the situation to develop after direct negotiations with Poland had broken down and while the Western powers were seeking to reach a settlement with Soviet Russia. Clear enough about his objectives, he contrived to keep his plans flexible. In the case of the annexation of Austria and of the occupation of Prague, he made the final decision on the spur of the moment.

Until he was convinced that the right moment had come Hitler would find a hundred excuses for procrastination. His hesitation in such cases was notorious: his refusal to make up his mind to stand as a presidential candidate in 1932, and his attempt to defer taking action against Röhm and the SA in 1934, are two obvious examples. Once he had made up his mind to move, however, he would act boldly, taking considerable risks, as in the reoccupation of the Rhineland in 1936, or the invasion of Norway and Denmark just before the major campaign in the west.

Surprise was a favorite gambit of Hitler's, in politics, diplomacy, and war: he gauged the psychological effect of sudden, unexpected hammer-blows in paralyzing opposition. An illustration of his appreciation of the value of surprise and quick decision, even when on the defensive, is the second presidential campaign of 1932. It had taken Goebbels weeks to persuade Hitler to stand for the presidency at all. The defeat in the first ballot brought Goebbels to despair; but Hitler, now that he had committed himself, with great presence of mind dictated the announcement that he would stand a second time and got it onto the streets almost before the country had learned of his defeat. In war the psychological effect of the blitzkrieg was just as important in Hitler's eyes as the strategic: it gave the impression that the German military machine was more than life-size, that it possessed some virtue of invincibility against which ordinary men could not defend themselves.

No regime in history has ever paid such careful attention to psychological factors in politics. Hitler was a master of mass emotion. To attend one of his big meetings was to go through an emotional experience, not to listen to an argument or a program. Yet nothing was left to chance on these occasions. Every device for heightening the emotional intensity, every trick of the theater was used. The Nuremberg rallies held every year in September were masterpieces of theatrical art, with the most carefully devised effects. "I had spent six years in St. Petersburg before the war in the best days of the old Russian ballet," wrote Sir Nevile Henderson, "but for grandiose beauty I have never seen a ballet to compare with it." To see the films of the Nuremberg rallies even today is to be recaptured by the hypnotic effect of thousands of men marching in perfect order, the music of the massed bands, the forest of standards and flags, the vast perspectives of the stadium, the smoking torches, the dome of searchlights. The sense of power, of force, and unity was irresistible, and all converged with a mounting crescendo of excitement on the supreme moment when the Führer himself made his entry. Paradoxically, the man who was most affected by such spectacles was their originator, Hitler himself, and, as Rosenberg remarks in his memoirs, they played an indispensable part in the process of self-intoxication.

Hitler had grasped as no one before him what could be done with a combination of propaganda and terrorism. For the complement to the attractive power of the great spectacles was the compulsive power of the Gestapo, the SS, and the concentration camp, heightened once again by skillful propaganda. Hitler was helped in this not only by his own perception of the sources of power in a modern urbanized mass society, but also by possession of the technical means to manipulate them. This was a point well made by Albert Speer, Hitler's highly intelligent minister for armaments and war production, in the final speech he made at his trial after the war.

> *Hitler's dictatorship [Speer told the court] differed in one fundamental point from all its predecessors in history. His was the first dictatorship in the present period of modern technical development, a dictatorship which made complete use of all technical means for the domination of its own country.*
>
> *Through technical devices like the radio and the loud-speaker, eighty million people were deprived of independent thought. It was thereby possible to subject them to the will of one man. . . .*
>
> *Earlier dictators needed highly qualified assistants, even at the lowest level, men who could think and act independently. The totalitarian system in the period of modern technical development can dispense with them; the means of communication alone make it possible to mechanize the lower leadership. As a result of this there arises the new type of the uncritical recipient of orders. . . . Another result was the far-reaching supervision of the citizens of the State and the maintenance of a high degree of secrecy for criminal acts.*
>
> *The nightmare of many a man that one day nations could be dominated by technical means was all but realized in Hitler's totalitarian system.*

In making use of the formidable power which was thus placed in his hands Hitler had one supreme, and fortunately rare, advantage: he had neither scruples nor inhibitions. He was a man without roots, with neither home nor family; a man who admitted no loyalties, was bound by no traditions, and felt respect neither for God nor man. Throughout his career Hitler showed himself prepared to seize any advantage that was to be gained by lying, cunning, treachery, and unscrupulousness. He demanded the sacrifice of millions of German lives for the sacred cause of Germany, but in the last year of the war was ready to destroy Germany rather than surrender his power or admit defeat.

Wary and secretive, he entertained a universal distrust. He admitted no one to his counsels. He never let down his guard, or gave himself away. "He never," Schacht wrote, "let slip an unconsidered word. He never said what he did not intend to say and he never blurted out a secret. Everything was the result of cold calculation.". . .

Cynical though he was, Hitler's cynicism stopped short of his own person: he came to believe that he was a man with a mission, marked out by Providence, and therefore exempt from the ordinary canons of human conduct.

Hitler probably held some such belief about himself from an early period. It was clear enough in the speech he made at his trial in 1924, and after he came out of prison those near him noticed that he began to hold aloof, to set a barrier between himself and his followers. After he came to power it became more noticeable. It was in March 1936 that he made the famous assertion already quoted: "I go the way that Providence dictates with the assurance of a sleep-walker." In 1937 he told an audience at Würzburg:

> *However weak the individual may be when compared with the omnipotence and will of Providence, yet at the moment when he acts as Providence would have him act he becomes immeasurably strong. Then there streams down upon him that force which has marked all greatness in the world's history. And when I look back only on the five years which lie behind us, then I feel that I am justified in saying: That has not been the work of man alone.*

Just before the occupation of Austria, in February 1938, he declared in the Reichstag:

> *Above all, a man who feels it his duty at such an hour to assume the leadership of his people is not responsible to the laws of parliamentary usage or to a particular democratic conception, but solely to the mission placed upon him. And anyone who interferes with this mission is an enemy of the people.*

It was in this sense of mission that Hitler, a man who believed neither in God nor in conscience ("a Jewish invention, a blemish like circumcision"), found both justification and absolution. He was the Siegfried come to reawaken Germany to greatness, for whom morality, suffering, and "the litany of private virtues" were irrelevant. It was by such dreams that he sustained the ruthlessness and determination of his will. So long as this sense of mission was balanced by the cynical calculations of the politician, it represented a source of strength, but success was fatal. When half Europe lay at his feet and all need of restraint was removed, Hitler abandoned himself entirely to megalomania. He became convinced of his own infallibility. But when he began to look to the image he had created to work miracles of its own accord — instead of exploiting it — his gifts deteriorated and his intuition deluded him. Ironically, failure sprang from the same capacity which brought him success, his power of self-dramatization, his ability to convince himself. His belief in his power to work miracles kept him going when the more skeptical Mussolini faltered. Hitler played out his "world-historical" role to the bitter end. But it was this same belief which curtained him in illusion and blinded him to what was actually happening, leading him into that arrogant overestimate of his own genius which brought him to defeat. The sin which Hitler committed was that which the ancient Greeks called hybris, the sin of overweening pride, of believing himself to be more than a man. No man was ever more surely destroyed by the image he had created than Adolf Hitler.

Ernst Nolte

Infantilism, Monomania, Mediumism

No one is likely to query the statement that Hitler was even more essential to National Socialism than Maurras was to the Action Française or Mussolini to Italian Fascism. He also did not create his movement from nothing, of course, and objective factors of great significance combined with a thousand favorable circumstances to work to his advantage; nevertheless, it is very much easier to imagine Fascism without Mussolini than National Socialism without Hitler.

The fact that right from the start Hitler was a more extreme figure than Mussolini or Maurras is accounted for only in small part by the circumstances and events of his youth. Indeed, there are as many analogies here as deviations.

In common with Maurras and Mussolini, Hitler came from the provincial lower middle class of a Catholic country, although he alone lived under the shadow of the dreaded unknown factor in his family history. He too had a nonbelieving father and a pious and beloved mother. At fourteen he also was a "freethinker," but, unlike Mussolini, he was not offered a coherent system of political faith as a substitute.

As a young man he went to the distant capital to devote himself to

From *Three Faces of Fascism*, by Ernst Nolte. Translated by Leila Vennewitz. Copyright © 1965 by R. Piper & Co. Reprinted by permission of the publisher and the author.

an artistic profession; in helpless rage he looked upon the strangeness around him, typified for him — as for Maurras — by the Jew. He became acquainted with poverty and even, like Mussolini, tried begging. But his ideas did not develop, as Maurras's did, under the critical eye of a literary public; he lectured on his weltanschauung to the inmates of men's hostels and shelters for the destitute; he did not, as did Mussolini, receive any vocational training. He left school early and lived for two years in his mother's house without a job; then, until he was twenty-five, he wandered around Vienna and Munich, eking out a meager living by painting postcards. The Dreyfus affair made a politician out of Maurras — a not entirely unknown writer who enjoyed the esteem of friends who were celebrities; World War I confronted Mussolini, a party leader of considerable standing, with the most important decision of his career; the war was a cataclysmic experience for Hitler too, but even though it brought him for the first time face to face with an overwhelming reality to which he enthusiastically responded, it merely cast him from the nothingness of bourgeois existence into the nothingness of the obscure common soldier, and when in 1918 he decided to enter politics the material foundation of his life was still nothingness.

The differences in the circumstances surrounding their lives were therefore not so much objective facts as the products of differing reactions. Maurras and Mussolini came to terms with the intellectual premises and random happenings of their lives with a similar prompt and clear-cut decisiveness. There were some things to which Hitler did not react at all — hence his inertia, his aimless drifting, his inconsistency — as against others which provoked an extremely sharp reaction. A psychological description of Maurras and Mussolini was superfluous; references to the outstanding intelligence and literary bent of the one, and the "impressionability" of the other, merely served to indicate normal characteristics intensified to a supranormal degree.

Hitler was different. In his case certain dominant traits came to the fore which, although they cannot immediately be dubbed "abnormal," did approach the abnormal and are best described in psychopathological terms. In view of the unchanging nature of character and convictions which Hitler shared with Maurras, it is permissible to cite examples . . . from all periods of his life.

The fact that, according to August Kubizek, the friend of his youth, Hitler's favorite stories were legends of German heroes, that he steeped himself in the world of those ancient times and identified himself with their heroes, was no doubt something he had in common with innumerable boys of his age. The fact that he designed a magnificent house in the Renaissance style for the woman he silently adored from afar merely put him on a level with a smaller group of young men. But that he should plan, down to the last detail, a luxurious apartment for himself and his friend in the firm hope of winning a lottery, that he should mentally engage an "exceptionally refined elderly lady" as receptionist and tutor for the two art students, that after the disillusionment of the lottery drawing he should passionately and in all seriousness inveigh against the lottery in particular and the world in general — this must have removed him some considerable distance from the majority of even the most fanciful of his age group.

Moreover, this extraordinary capacity for wishful thinking, this mingling of reality and dream, did not diminish with time. Scarcely had one of his companions in a Vienna men's hostel described certain technical plans, of direct concern to him as a future engineer, than Hitler already saw himself part owner of the firm "Greiner & Hitler, Airplane Construction." In *Hitler's Table Talk* (published in America as *Hitler's Secret Conversations*), Hitler speaks of the poverty of that period of his life. "But in my imagination I dwelled in palaces." It was during that time, he said, that he drew up the first plans for the remodeling of Berlin.

There are many witnesses to the fact that during his time of struggle he was already living in the Third Reich, untouched by doubts of any kind, impervious to counsels of moderation, devoid of any desire for sober assessment and calculation. Hermann Rauschning's *Gespräche mit Hitler* provide what is probably the most vivid picture of the utter lack of restraint of this inordinate imagination.

When he was in the throes of remodeling Berlin and Linz, his plans were far from exhausted. The new Reich Chancellery had to be so vast that all would recognize it immediately as the seat of the "master of the world," and by comparison St. Peter's would seem a mere toy. No turn of events in the war could shake the power of this desire, this vision, nor was its force of conviction affected by the fact that this dream was just as divorced from reality as it had been during his youth.

In January 1945, the Gauleiter of Danzig came to Hitler, disheartened and full of defiant resolve to confront Hitler with the whole truth about the desperate situation of his city. He left the room, according to the secretary, a changed man, miraculously cheered and encouraged: the Führer had promised him relief. There was no relief anywhere in sight, but Hitler saw it in his mind's eye and was able to convince a man with perfect vision that he was blind.

As late as March 1945, his secretary saw him standing interminably in front of the wooden model of the future city of Linz. He was still dreaming the dreams of his youth.

The dominant trait in Hitler's personality was infantilism. It explains the most prominent as well as the strangest of his characteristics and actions. The frequently awesome consistency of his thoughts and behavior must be seen in conjunction with the stupendous force of his rage, which reduced field marshals to trembling nonentities. If at the age of fifty he built the Danube bridge in Linz down to the last detail exactly as he had designed it at the age of fifteen before the eyes of his astonished boyhood friend, this was not a mark of consistency in a mature man, one who has learned and pondered, criticized and been criticized, but the stubbornness of the child who is aware of nothing except himself and his mental image and to whom time means nothing because childishness has not been broken and forced into the sober give-and-take of the adult world. Hitler's rage was the uncontrollable fury of the child who bangs the chair because the chair refuses to do as it is told; his dreaded harshness, which nonchalantly sent millions of people to their death, was much closer to the rambling imaginings of a boy than to the iron grasp of a man, and is therefore intimately and typically related to his profound aversion to the cruelty of hunting, vivisection, and the consumption of meat generally.

And how close to the sinister is the grotesque! The first thing Hitler did after being released from the Landsberg prison was to buy a Mercedes for 26,000 marks — the car he had been dreaming of while serving his sentence. Until 1933 he insisted on passing every car on the road. In Vienna alone he had heard *Tristan and Isolde* between thirty and forty times, and had time as chancellor to see six performances of *The Merry Widow* in as many months. Nor was this all. According to Otto Dietrich he reread all Karl May's boys' adventure books during 1933 and 1934, and this is perfectly credible since in *Hitler's Table Talk* he bestowed high praise on this author and credited him with no less than opening his eyes to the world. It is in the conversations related in *Hitler's Table Talk* that he treated his listeners to such frequent and vindictive schoolboy reminiscences that it seems as if this man never emerged from his boyhood and completely lacked the experience of time and its broadening, reconciling powers.

The monomaniacal element in Hitler's nature is obviously closely related to his infantilism. It is based largely on his elemental urge toward tangibility, intelligibility, simplicity. In *Mein Kampf* he expressed the maxim that the masses should never be shown more than *one* enemy. He was himself the most loyal exponent of this precept, and not from motives of tactical calculation alone. He never allowed himself to face more than one enemy at a time; on this enemy he concentrated all the hatred of which he was so inordinately capable, and it was this that enabled him during this period to show the other enemies a reassuring and "subjectively" sincere face. During the crisis in Czechoslovakia he even forgot the Jews over Beneš. His enemy was always concrete and personal, never merely the expression but also the cause of an obscure or complex event. The Weimar system was caused by the "November criminals," the predicament of the Germans in Austria by the Habsburgs, capitalism and Bolshevism equally by the Jews.

A good example of the emergence and function of the clearly defined hate figure, which took the place of the causal connection he really had in mind, is to be found in *Mein Kampf*. Here Hitler draws a vivid picture of the miseries of proletarian existence as he came to know it in Vienna — deserted, frustrated, devoid of hope. This description seems to lead inevitably to an obvious conclusion: that these people, if they were not wholly insensible, were bound to be led with compelling logic to the socialist doctrine, to their "lack of patriotism," their hatred of religion, their merciless indictment of the ruling class. It should, however, have also led to a self-critical insight: that the only reason he remained so aloof from the collective emotions of these masses was because he had enjoyed a different upbringing, middle-class and provincial, because despite his poverty he never really worked, and because he was not married. Nothing of the kind! When he was watching spellbound one day as the long column of demonstrating workers wound its way through the streets, his first query was about the "wirepullers." His voracity for reading, his allegedly thorough study of Marxist theories, did not spur him on to cast his gaze beyond the frontier and realize that such demonstrations were taking place in every city in Europe, or to take note of the "rabble-rousing" articles of a certain Mussolini, which he would doubtless have regarded as "spiritual vitriol" like those in the *Arbeiterzeitung*.

France Is Defeated. Hitler dances a merry jig after receiving the capitulation of French officials in the famous railway car at Compiègne, where Germany had been forced to surrender in 1918. Revenge was sweet for the Nazis in 1940, but the war was far from over. (Wide World Photos)

What Hitler discovered was the many Jewish names among the leaders of Austrian Marxism, and now the scales fell from his eyes — at last he saw who it was who, besides the Habsburgs, wanted to wipe out the German element in Austria. Now he began to preach his conclusions to his first audiences; now he was no longer speaking, as until recently he had spoken to Kubizek, to hear the sound of his own voice: he wanted to convince. But he did not have much success. The management of the men's hostel looked on him as an insufferable politicizer, and for most of his fellow inmates he was a "reactionary swine." He got beaten up by workers, and in conversations with Jews and Social Democrats he was evidently often the loser, being no match for their diabolical glibness and dialectic. This made the image of the archenemy appear all the more vivid to him, all the more firmly entrenched. Thirty years later the most experienced statesmen took him for a confidence-inspiring statesman after meeting him personally; hard-bitten soldiers found he was a man they could talk to; educated supporters saw in him the people's social leader. Hitler himself, however, made the following observations in the presence of the generals and party leaders around his table: though Dietrich Eckart had considered that from many aspects Streicher was a fool, it was impossible to conquer the masses without such people, . . . though Streicher was criticized for his paper, *Der Stürmer;* in actual fact Streicher idealized the Jew. The Jew was far more ignoble, unruly, and diabolical than Streicher had depicted him.

Hitler rose from the gutter to be the master of Europe. There is no doubt that he learned an enormous amount. In the flexible outer layer of his personality he could be all things to all men: a statesman to the statesmen, a commander to the generals, a charmer to women, a father to the people. But in the hard monomaniacal core of his being he did not change one iota from Vienna to Rastenburg.

Yet if his people had found that he intended after the war to prohibit smoking and make the world of the future vegetarian it is probable that even the SS would have rebelled. There are thousands of monomaniacal and infantile types in every large community, but they seldom play a role other than among their own kind. These two traits do not explain how Hitler was able to rise to power.

August Kubizek tells a strange story which there is little reason to doubt and which sheds as much light on the moment when Hitler decided to enter politics as on the basis and prospects of that decision. After a performance of *Rienzi* in Linz, Kubizek relates, Hitler had taken him up to a nearby hill and talked to him with shining eyes and trembling voice of the mandate he would one day receive from his people to lead them out of servitude to the heights of liberty. It seemed as if another self were speaking from Hitler's lips, as if he himself were looking on at what was happening in numb astonishment. Here the infantile basis is once again unmistakable. The identification with the hero of the dramatic opera bore him aloft, erupted from him like a separate being. There were many subsequent occasions testifying to this very process. When Hitler chatted, his manner of talking was often unbearably flat; when he described something, it was dull; when he theorized, it was stilted; when he started up a hymn of hate, repulsive. But time and again his speeches contained passages of irresistible force and compelling conviction, such as no other speaker of his time was capable of producing. These are always the places where his "faith" finds expression, and it was obviously this faith which induced that emotion among the masses to which even the most hostile observer testified. But at no time do these passages reveal anything new, never do they make the listener reflect or exert his critical faculty: all they ever do is conjure up magically before his eyes that which already existed in him as vague feeling, inarticulate longing. What else did he express but the secret desires of his judges when he declared before the People's Court: "The army we have trained is growing day by day, faster by the hour. It is in these very days that I have the proud hope that the hour will come when these unruly bands become battalions, the battalions regiments, the regiments divisions, when the old cockade is raised from the dust, when the old flags flutter again on high, when at last reconciliation takes place before the eternal Last Judgment, which we are prepared to face."

His behavior at a rally has often been described: how, uncertain at first, he would rely on the trivial, then get the feel of the atmosphere for several minutes, slowly establish contact, score a bull's-eye with the right phrase, gather momentum with the applause, finally burst out with words which seemed positively to erupt through him, and at the end, in the midst of thunderous cheering, shout a vow to heaven or, amid breathless silence, bring forth a solemn Amen. And after the speech he was as wet as if he had taken a steambath and had lost as much weight as if he had been through a week's strict training.

He told every rally what it wanted to hear — yet what he voiced was not the trivial interests and desires of the day but the great universal, obvious hopes: that Germany should once again become what it had been, that the economy should function, that the farmer should get his rights, likewise the townsman, the worker, and the employer, that they should forget their differences and become one in the most important thing of all — their love for Germany. He never embarked on discussion, he permitted no heckling, he never dealt with any of the day-to-day problems of politics. When he knew that a rally was in a critical mood and wanted information instead of weltanschauung, he was capable of calling off his speech at the last moment.

There should be no doubt as to the mediumistic trait in Hitler. He was the medium who communicated to the masses their own, deeply buried spirit. It was because of this, not because of his monomaniacal obsession, that a third of his people loved him long before he became chancellor, long before he was their victorious supreme commander. But mediumistic popular idols are usually simpletons fit for ecstasy rather than fulfillment. In the turmoil of postwar Germany it would have been *impossible* to love Hitler had not monomaniacal obsession driven the man on and infantile wishful thinking carried him beyond the workaday world with its problems and conflicts. Singly, any one of these three characteristics would have made Hitler a freak and a fool; combined, they raised him for a brief time to be lord and master of his troubled era.

A psychological portrait of Hitler such as this must, however, give rise to doubts in more ways than one. Does the portrait not approach that overpolemical and oversimplified talk of the "madman" or the "criminal"? There is no intention of claiming that this represents a clinical diagnosis. It is not even the purpose of this analysis to define and categorize Hitler as an "infantile mediumistic monomaniac." What has been discussed is merely the existence of infantile, mediumistic, and monomaniacal traits. They are not intended to exhaust the nature of the man Hitler, nor do they of themselves belong to the field of the medically abnormal. Rather do they represent individually an indispensable ingredient of the exceptional. There can be few artists without a streak of infantilism, few ideological politicians without a monomaniacal element in their make-up. It is not so much the potency of each element singly as the combination of all three which gives Hitler his unique face. Whether this combination is pathological in the clinical sense is very doubtful, but there can be no doubt that it excludes historical greatness in the traditional sense.

A second objection is that the psychological description prevents the sociological typification which from the point of view of history is so much more productive. Many attempts have been made to understand Hitler as typical of the angry petit bourgeois. The snag in this interpretation is that it cannot stand without a psychologizing adjective and almost always suggests a goal which is obviously psychological as well as polemical. What this theory tries to express is that Hitler was "actually only a petit bourgeois," in other words, something puny and contemptible. But it is precisely from the psychological standpoint that the petit bourgeois can best be defined as the normal image of the "adult": Hitler was exactly the reverse. What is correct, however, is that, from the sociological standpoint, bourgeois elements may be present in an entirely nonbourgeois psychological form. It remains to be shown how very petit bourgeois was Hitler's immediate reaction to Marxism. However, it was only by means of that "form" which cannot be deduced by sociological methods that his first reaction underwent its momentous transformation.

The third objection is the most serious. The historical phenomenon of National Socialism might be considered overparticularized if it is based solely on the unusual, not to say abnormal, personality of one man. Does not this interpretation in the final analysis even approach that all too transparent apologia which tries to see in Hitler, and only in him, the "*causa efficiens* of the whole sequence of events"? But this is not necessarily logical. It is only from one aspect that the infantile person is more remote from the world than other people; from another aspect he is much closer to it. For he does not dredge up the stuff of his dreams and longings out of nothing; on the contrary, he compresses the world of his more normal fellow men, sometimes by intensifying, sometimes by contrasting. From the complexity of life, monomaniacal natures often wrest an abstruse characteristic, quite frequently a comical aspect, but at times a really essential element. However, the mediumistic trait guarantees that nothing peripheral is compressed, nothing trivial monomaniacally grasped. It is not that a nature of this kind particularizes the historical, but that this nature is itself brought into focus by the historical. Although far from being a true mirror of the times — indeed, it is more of a monstrous distortion — nothing goes into it that is pure invention; and what does go into it arises from certain traits of its own. Hitler sometimes compared himself to a magnet which attracted all that was brave and heroic; it would probably be more accurate to say that certain extreme characteristics of the era attracted this nature like magnets, to become in that personality even more extreme and visible. Hence . . . there[should] be little mention of Hitler's psyche, but all the more of the conditions, forces, and trends of his environment to which he stood in some relationship. For whether he merely interpreted these conditions or intervened in them, whether he placed himself on the side of these forces or opposed them, whether he let himself be borne along by these trends or fought them: something of this force or this trend never failed to emerge in extreme form. In this sense Hitler's nature may be called a historical substance.

Robert G. L. Waite

Guilt Feelings and Perverted Sexuality

A major problem in dealing with the life of Adolf Hitler is that of determining the extent to which he had confidence in himself as a person and as a political leader. This essay will discuss one aspect of his remarkably complex personality and will show that one of history's most ruthless rulers was beset by feelings of guilt and the need for self-punishment.

In public and private speech, Hitler revealed his concern by talking repeatedly about unworthiness, guilt, and conscience. He worried, for example, about his own worthiness in the sight of God and attempted to quiet his doubts in two ways. He protested too much that he really was worthy, saying, typically, "The Great Judge of all time . . . will always give victory to those who are the most worthy [*würdig*]." And again, "I carry my heavy burdens with dutiful thanks to Providence which has deemed me *worthy*. . . ." Another way of silencing his own doubts was to insist that, while he certainly was worthy, others were not. Thus the Jews were unworthy to be citizens of his Reich and must die. By 1945 he reached the conclusion that the entire German people had proved unworthy of him; they too should perish.

Over and over again he showed that he was bothered by conscience and felt the need of dulling its demands:

> *Only when the time comes when the race is no longer overshadowed by the* consciousness of its own guilt *then will it find internal peace.*

> Conscience *is a Jewish invention. It is a blemish like circumcision.* . . .

> *I am freeing men from* . . . *the* dirty *and degrading modification of a chimera called* conscience and morality.

> *We must distrust the intelligence and the* conscience. . . .

Reprinted without footnotes from *The Journal of Interdisciplinary History*, I (1971), 229–249, with the permission of the editors of *The Journal of Interdisciplinary History* and The MIT Press, Cambridge, Massachusetts. © 1971 by The Massachusetts Institute of Technology and the editors of *The Journal of Interdisciplinary History*.

> *We must be ruthless . . . we must regain our* clear conscience *as to ruthlessness. . . . Only thus shall we* purge *our people.*

Hitler was even convinced that dogs suffer from a "bad conscience."

The Führer felt guilty about something. But when a historian attempts to give the precise reasons for those guilt feelings, he is reminded again of Trevelyan's trenchant admonition to those who would try to make of history a science: "in the most important part of its business, history is . . . an imaginative guess."

Aided by the insights of psychoanalysis, let us set forth here our best guesses as to the causes of Hitler's feelings of guilt. One possibility can quickly be eliminated. Hitler felt no remorse whatever over the calculated murder of millions of "racially inferior" people, or the holocaust of war, or the annihilation of the village of Lidice, or the planned destruction of the Fatherland and the burning of Paris, or the squandered lives of young German soldiers. Atrocities did not disturb Hitler. Other guesses are needed.

Hitler seems to have felt unworthy of being the Führer of a racially pure Germany because he suspected that he himself might have been "guilty of having Jewish blood" — as the barbarous expression ran in the Third Reich. He had been so shaken in 1930 when he heard dark hints that his own grandfather might have been a Jew that he sent his personal lawyer, Hans Frank, to investigate. Frank's report was not reassuring. It said that Hitler's father was born out of wedlock to a certain Maria Anna Schicklgruber who had worked as a domestic in Graz, Austria, "in the home of a Jewish family by the name of Frankenberger." That Frank's investigations may have been in error does not alter the crucial fact that Hitler *believed that they might be correct* and was haunted by the fear that he himself might be "part Jewish." He testified to this fear in various ways. He took special pains to dictate the precise language of the Nuremberg Racial Laws of 1935 and gave orders that not one word should be changed. The wording of Article 3 is particularly interesting. Of all the civil disabilities for Jews he might have ordered, he set forth this one: "Jews may not employ female household servants of German or related blood who are under 45 years of age." Hitler's own grandmother had been forty-two when she gave birth to Hitler's father.

Anxiety about a Jewish grandfather was also shown when he projected his own fears onto Matthias Erzberger, a leader of the Center party whom Hitler accused of betraying Germany by accepting the Versailles treaty: "Matthias Erzberger . . . *the illegitimate son of a servant girl and a Jewish employer,* was the German negotiator who set his name to the document which had the deliberate intention of bringing about the destruction of Germany." The servant girl in a Jewish household was still on his mind years later. In one of his nightly monologues during 1942 he told his entourage about "a country girl who had a place in Nuremberg in the household of Herr Hirsch," who had raped her.

Hitler projected guilt feelings about the impurity of his own blood in another way. He sought to lessen his personal anxiety by universalizing the guilt, saying that all Germans were at fault. Thus he insisted that "*All of us* are suffering from . . . mixed, corrupted blood. How can we purify ourselves and make atonement?"

There is further evidence that Hitler suspected his own blood was tainted. Just two months after taking over Austria in March 1938, Hitler had a survey made of the lovely little farming village of Döllersheim — the village where his father had been born and his grandmother buried. The purpose of the survey was to determine the suitability of the area for an artillery range for the Germany army. The commanding general of Wehrkreis XVII was given orders directly from Hitler to make the area ready "as soon as possible" for that purpose. The inhabitants were evacuated, the village was demolished by artillery fire, and the graves of the cemetery were rendered unrecognizable. Why? There are thousands of empty acres in this part of Lower Austria. Hitler must have chosen this particular village as an artillery range because he felt a great compulsion to wipe out — quite literally — the suspicion of his own Jewish blood by obliterating the birthplace of his father and the grave of his grandmother whom he considered guilty of contaminating him.

In the so-called "Gestapo Reports" of the Main Archives of the party, there are records of several separate investigations of Hitler's own family background. The most thorough of these inquiries was made in 1942 — just prior to the onset of the massacres which killed about 6 million Jews. Why were these special investigations undertaken? Hitler rarely talked about his own family. Why then did he have this remarkable concern about his ancestors unless he was anxiously hoping to prove that he was a "pure Aryan" — or at least as Aryan as his own racial laws required?

Hitler also manifested his concern about "racial contamination" in both his public and private life. Racial purity was, of course, absolutely basic to the whole theory of National Socialism, and in public speeches he often spoke about "blood baths," "the blood order," and "the blood flag." But his concern about blood went beyond that. He worried about his own blood and seems to have been convinced that there was something wrong with it. He became a vegetarian partly because he thought that a vegetable diet would purify his blood. And he regularly got rid of his blood by letting leeches suck it from him. Later, his quack doctor, Theodor Morell, drew it from him, and preserved it in test tubes, so that Hitler could gaze at it apprehensively.

The feeling that his own blood was impure contributed to his sense of unworthiness and inadequacy in performing the role of mighty Führer of a racially pure Reich. Hence he often looked anxiously into a mirror and asked his valet for assurance, saying, "I really do look like the Führer. Don't I, Linge?" As a young man he had been teased about looking Jewish, and the suggestion continued to bother him.

Hitler also seems to have felt guilty about incestuous desires. His relations with both his mother and his niece were very close indeed, and the word incest was often on his mind. Whether or not he actually acted out his incestuous feelings is not very important psychologically. As Freud showed us long ago, fantasies can be as psychically formative as realities.

It is also possible that acute feelings of unworthiness, guilt, and self-loathing were a consequence of a massively masochistic sexual perversion. Hitler gained sexual satisfaction by having a young woman — as much younger than he as his mother was younger than his father — squat over him to urinate or defecate on his head.

When confronted with data such as these, a biographer of Adolf Hitler has at least three options. He can ignore such evidence as sensational, embarrassing, and quite beneath the dignity of a serious historian. He can use some of the data selectively as unusual sidelights, showing the eccentricities of his subject. Or he can try to show how a discussion of Hitler's psychological abnormalities had historical consequences and can help in a fuller understanding of him as a person. With appropriate trepidation — and trepidation is certainly appropriate here — let us suggest some historical results in Hitler's personal feelings of guilt and unworthiness.

Most obviously, he sought relief from his burden of guilt by an elaborate system of defenses. Indeed he displayed virtually all the major mechanisms Anna Freud has described in her classical work on the subject. He relied heavily, for example, upon reaction formation. Thus his perversion and voyeurism were masked behind ostentatiously prudish behavior. He appeared a moral and ascetic person who forbade the telling of off-color stories in his presence, who did not swear, who denied himself alcohol and tobacco, and who objected when women wore lipstick. He complained that it was manufactured from French urine. He showed that he was disturbed by the filth of his perversion in the number of times the words urine, filth, and dirt were on his mind, saying, typically, that he would free men from "the dirty and degrading" aspects of conscience, or that Jews were "filthy," "unclean," "like a maggot in a rotting corpse." His reaction formation against filth was appropriately extreme and took the form of excessive cleanliness. He washed his hair at least once a day, bathed and changed his underwear twice daily, and scrubbed his hands frequently. He was greatly concerned about his body odors. One of the reasons he became a vegetarian was because — like Benjamin Franklin — he believed that eating meat increased the objectionable odor of flatulation, a chronic complaint of Hitler's which he sought to alleviate by taking enormous quantities of "Dr. Köster's Antigas Pills." These efforts to make his body odors less objectionable were linked to his fear that he might be part Jewish. Jews, he insisted, had a peculiar and objectionable odor.

Hitler also sought to lessen his feelings of guilt through self-punishment — hence his abstentious habits and the masochism of his perversion. It is even conceivable that he actually punished himself physically to the point of partial self-castration. And time and again he promised to commit suicide, the ultimate masochistic dissolution. Among the many childish games he played was a form of substitute suicide. Hitler disliked tying his own necktie and ordered his valet to do it for him. He would hold his breath during the process and count slowly to ten. If Linge could finish the knot before Hitler had finished counting, the Führer was greatly relieved.

Adolf Hitler also indulged in a form of self-punishment which may have had important historical consequences. As McRandle was first to suggest, Hitler punished himself by unconscious desires for failure and defeat. Of course, his life can be seen quite differently, as a remarkable success story, with an unlikely hero played by a neurotic dropout of Linz and Vienna who had failed in all his undertakings and been jailed at the start of his political career, but who, within a decade, became the master of Germany and then arbiter of Europe. Historians are clearly justified in dwelling on Hitler's extraordinary gifts and brilliant victories. And yet there is a curious pattern of behavior that also needs to be noted in attempting to understand this very complex personality. Throughout his life, Adolf Hitler flirted with failure and involved himself unnecessarily in situations that were fraught with danger to himself and his movement.

During his first years in elementary school, Adolf had had an excellent record, but he failed to get a diploma from Realschule and ran away to Vienna. He failed his first examination for the academy of art, and, when given a second chance, he did not apply himself and failed a second time. His first bid for power in 1923 shows a similar pattern of choosing the alternatives least likely to succeed. Throughout the summer of 1923 he made no plans for seizing political power. He gratuitously insulted the leading military figures of Bavaria and Germany, Generals Franz Ritter von Epp, Otto von Lossow, and Hans von Seeckt — men whose support or neutrality was indispensable to him if he planned a coup. Having failed to make preparations, he suddenly called forth a great national revolution which had no chance of success, loudly promising either total victory or suicide. Instead, he ran away and hid in the summer home of a Harvard graduate, "Putzi" Hanfstaengl. Arrested and confronted by political disaster, he extricated himself by brilliant demogoguery.

Hitler's record during the "seizure of power" in 1920–1933 is usually considered brilliant, perhaps because it was successful. And surely there were signs of both enormous energy and political acumen. But there is also evidence of political mistakes so glaring as to suggest an unconscious desire for failure. He went out of his way, for example, to alienate the one great political force he needed to mollify, and ran for the presidency against President Field-Marshal Paul von Hindenburg. Hitler's success in 1933 was due at least as much to the stupidities and failures of Weimar's political leaders as it was to his own efforts.

Similarly, however one interprets his foreign policy, it can be viewed as an invitation to disaster. Three differing interpretations may be considered. First, if A. J. P. Taylor is right in insisting that all Hitler really wanted was a negotiated revision of Versailles, then the methods he employed to attain that end were indeed "singularly inappropriate." Second, if we are to suppose that Hitler wanted only a limited war against Poland to gain Danzig and the corridor, certainly his bellicose speeches against the Western powers, his atrocities against the Jews and other minorities, and his broken promises to Chamberlain show him proceeding in ways unlikely to isolate Poland and most likely to assure his victim of strong allies. Finally, let us suppose he really plotted the great war of European conquest that he had promised in *Mein Kampf,* again in 1925, in his second book of 1928, and in a dozen speeches. If so, he made inadequate preparations for fighting such a war. He got himself involved in a general conflict against the Western powers and still promised total victory or total destruction. Once more, largely through intuition, skill, and luck, he was victorious in the West. Then he decided to attack Russia at the very time that it was trying desperately to appease him by shipping Germany thousands of tons of supplies. While his offensive against the USSR faltered and failed, Hitler suddenly declared war on the United States, the greatest industrial power on earth. Thus it was Hitler who took the initiative in bringing about the kind of global war he could not conceivably win. And during those titanic years from 1941–1944 Hitler dawdled and dithered over the crucial question of a war economy for Germany. Economic mobilization was not really declared until the autumn of 1944, that is, until well after "Fortress Europa" had been breached from the West and Russia was counterattacking along a thousand miles of the Eastern front. Only then, when it was much too late, did Hitler hesitatingly move in the direction of full economic mobilization. But he could never bring himself to give clear orders for a complete war economy.

In the end, as he had done so often in his life, he ran away and hid, this time in his air-raid shelter in Berlin. He killed himself by taking poison and having his bride perform the coup de grâce.

Throughout his career, Hitler seldom contemplated a line of action without thinking of defeat. The disjunctives which characterized his thought almost invariably included the possibility of failure and of suicide. Typically, in the midst of the Beer Hall Putsch, he turned to Gustav von Kahr, Lossow, and Hans von Seisser and said, "You must be victorious with me or die with me. If things go wrong, I have four bullets in my pistol: three for my fellow workers if they desert me, the last bullet is for me." He contemplated failure and suicide on many other occasions: while hiding at the Hanfstaengl summer home in 1923; upon his arrival in 1924 at Landsberg; in 1931 after the suicide of his niece, "Geli" Raubal; in 1932 if he were not appointed chancellor; in

1936 if the occupation of the Rhineland failed; and on many other occasions.

Even at the very height of prewar success he was concerned about failure. On November 10, 1938, for example, he addressed the German press in what should have been a moment of triumph. His first big pogrom against the Jews in the *Kristallnacht* had been executed with the acquiescence of the German people. During the preceding months he had enjoyed a series of other victories: the reintroduction of universal military training; the reoccupation of the Rhineland; the highly success- ful plebiscite approving his withdrawal from the League of Nations; Anschluss with Austria; and most recently the triumph of the Munich agreement. And yet his speech of November 10 is studded with foreboding. The words *Angst, Rückschlag, Niederlage,* and *Misserfolg* were very much on his mind:

> *I must tell you that I often have one single* misgiving . . . *I become almost* anxious. . . . *I have had nothing but successes, but what would happen if I were to suffer a* failure? *Yes, Gentlemen, even that can happen. . . . How would [the masses] act if we ever had a* failure? *Formerly, Gentlemen, it was my greatest pride that I built up a party that* even in time of defeat *stood behind me. . . .*

Certainly in sending first his lawyer and then the Gestapo to inves- tigate the racial purity of his own family he was taking an enormous risk. Psychologically he had based his very identity as a person on the projection of his own feelings of guilt, inadequacy, failure, and perver- sion onto the Jews; politically, he had staked his entire career on the principle of Aryan superiority and the terrible threat of the "Jewish Peril" from which he was defending Western civilization. If his investi- gators had found that Hitler's own grandfather had been a Jew, he could have been ruined by this disaster to both his psyche and his life work.

Incidents surrounding the launching of World War II also suggest preoccupation with prospects of failure. Albert Speer recalls that on the night of August 24, 1939, when Hitler's pact with Stalin — which gave him a free hand to attack the West — was announced, the Führer met with a small group of intimates at his "Eagle's Nest" overlooking Berchtesgaden. The group stood out on the balcony to watch a spec- tacular display of northern lights as they pulsated and throbbed above the Bavarian Alps. The dominant color was red, and the skies and mountains and the faces and hands of the watchers were washed in scarlet. Hitler saw an omen in the eery and foreboding light. He turned apprehensively to his military aide and said: "This time *we won't make it* without using force."

The complexities and contradictions of Hitler's personality are shown clearly in his conduct of the war. He displayed a great capacity for innovation in his use of armor and airpower; and his military campaigns against Poland and the West were smashing triumphs. Further, Hitler's successes as a tactician were, in the early years of the war, matched by remarkable strategic insight. Indeed, a distinguished British military analyst has concluded that "no strategist in history has been more clever in playing on the minds of his opponents — which is the supreme art of strategy."

All this is true. Hitler, it bears repeating, could act with devastating effectiveness, and his military abilities and victories should not be disparaged. Yet here too are suggestions that his remarkable career was beset by unconscious desires to punish himself in the very midst of success. There was the curious refusal to press his advantage at Dunkirk. There was the long hesitation and inaction after the fall of France — a time when "the wave of conquest broke on the shoals of delay and indecision." Month after month during the critical summer of 1940, Hitler continued to violate the cardinal principle of Clausewitz, an authority he had studied so avidly: "Once the great victory is gained there should be no talk of rest, of getting breath, or of consolidation, etc., but only of pursuit . . . of attacking. . . . "

Instead of concentrating his forces against his only remaining enemy, an isolated and desperately wounded England, Hitler turned to court his Nemesis. He sent his armies — without winter issue — marching into Russia. That he set the date for invasion in 1941 on the precise anniversary of Napoleon's ill-fated campaign (June 22) is perhaps coincidental, but why did he choose the code name of "Barbarossa"? It is true that Hitler saw himself, like Frederick Barbarossa, as a crusader whose mission it was to destroy an infidel Eastern enemy; but, as an avid reader of history, Hitler knew that the most notable thing about Barbarossa was that he was a failure. He had failed in five campaigns against the Lombard towns; he had failed to centralize the Holy Roman Empire; he had failed to obtain his objectives during the Third Crusade. And he had died by drowning. Adolf Hitler was pathologically afraid of the water, and had nightmares about loss of breath and strangulation. Moreover, the words Hitler used in announcing the invasion of Russia are worth remembering. "The world," he said, "will hold its breath." When Adolf Hitler held his breath and counted to ten while his valet tied his tie, he was symbolically enacting suicide and self-destruction.

Hitler also sought to dull his feelings of guilt by a kind of "introjection" in which he took upon himself the role of a great moral and religious leader. He saw himself as a messiah who was establishing a new religion and leading a great crusade against the cosmic forces of evil, that is, the incarnate evil of "the international Jewish conspiracy." It is not surprising, therefore, to find Hitler very seriously comparing himself to Jesus. He said on one occasion, as he lashed about him with a whip, "In driving out the Jews I remind myself of Jesus in the temple"; and on another, "Like Christ, I have a duty to my own people. . . . " He considered himself betrayed by Ernst Röhm in 1934 and drew the analogy to the betrayal of Jesus, saying, "Among the twelve apostles, there was also a Judas. . . . "

That he saw himself as the special agent of God and identified with Him was made manifest on many occasions:

I go the way that Providence dictates for me with all the assurance of a sleepwalker.

God has created this people and it has grown according to His will. And according to our will [nach unserem Willen] *it shall remain and never shall it pass away.*

I believe that it was God's will that from her [Austria] *a boy was sent into the Reich and that he grew up to become the Leader of the nation.*

By warding off the Jews, I am fighting for the Lord's work.

Hitler patterned the organization of his party and his Reich after the Roman Catholic church, which had impressed him so much as a young boy. He saw himself as a political pope with an apostolic succession when he announced to a closed meeting of the faithful in the Brown House during 1930, "I hereby set forth for myself and my successors in the leadership of the National Socialist Democratic Party the claim of political infallibility. I hope the world will grow as accustomed to that claim as it has to the claim of the Holy Father." The oath of direct obedience to the Führer was strikingly reminiscent of the special oath the Jesuits swore to the pope, and Hitler spoke of his elite SS, who wore the sacred ⚡⚡ and dressed in black, as a Society of Jesus, from which, he said, he had learned so much.

The bolts of excommunication and anathema which Hitler hurled against nonbelievers and heretics were not unlike those of a Gregory VII:

> *Woe to them who do not believe. These people have sinned . . . against all of life. . . . It is a miracle of faith that Germany has been saved. Today more than ever it is the duty of the Party to remember this National Socialist Confession of Faith* [Glaubensbekenntnis] *and to bear it forward as our holy* [heiliges] *sign of our battle and our victory.*

Hitler chose a cross as the symbol and sign of his movement.

The Nazis, like the Catholics, had their prophets, saints, and martyrs. Hitler's followers who fell during the Beer Hall Putsch were sanctified by Hitler when he said, in dedicating their memorial, that their death would bring forth "a true belief in the Resurrection of their people . . . the blood that they shed has become the baptismal water of the Third Reich." The annual Nazi march on November 9 from the Bürgerbraükeller to the Feldherrnhalle was a studied reenactment of the stations of the cross combined with the Passion Play. The analogy was made clear by the stress on "the blood that was shed for the redemption of the Fatherland."

Hitler's holy reliquary was the Brown House which contained the sacred Blood Flag which had been born by the martyrs of November 9. It was Hitler and Hitler alone who could perform the priestly ritual of touching the Blood Flag to the standards of the Brownshirts.

Hitler substituted Nazi high holy days for traditional religious holidays. They included January 30, the day Hitler came to power in the year he referred to as "the Holy Year of our Lord, 1933," and April 20, the leader's own birthday and the day when the Hitler Youth were confirmed in the faith. The holiest day, however, and one which served as a kind of Nazi Good Friday was November 9, celebrated as the Blood Witness [*Blutzeugen*] of the movement.

Religions require devils. For National Socialism, the Jewish people played that part, and Hitler insisted that the German people could achieve salvation only after they had destroyed the Jew who was, in

Hitler's words, *"the personification of the Devil"* and the "symbol of all evil." The concept was made unmistakably vivid in the childish rhyme:

> *Wer kennt den Jude*
> *Kennt den Teufel.*

Hitler also provided a sacred book for his new religion, and *Mein Kampf* replaced the Bible as the traditional wedding present given to all young Aryans. The close parallel between Christian commitment to God and the sacred oath of allegiance to Hitler is best seen in a description of public oath-taking recorded in the Nazi newspaper, *Westdeutscher Beobachter:* "Yesterday witnessed the profession of the Religion of the Blood in all its imposing reality. . . . Whoever has sworn his oath of allegiance to Hitler has pledged himself unto death to this sublime idea."

It is true that Hitler sometimes told his intimates that he did not wish to be deified, but he did little to stop his followers from exalting him as savior and messiah. Indeed, he directly approved the patent paganism and Führer worship of the Warthegau church as a model for the church he planned after the war. And he did not object to the following version of the Lord's Prayer which was recited by the League of German Girls:

> *Adolf Hitler, you are our great leader*
> *Thy name makes the enemy tremble.*
> *Thy Third Reich comes, thy will alone is law*
> *upon earth. Let us hear daily thy voice and*
> *order us by thy leadership, for we will obey*
> *to the end, even with our lives.*
> *We praise thee! Heil Hitler!*

It is to be noted that prayers were given not only for the Führer, but to him as a deity.

In speeches and soliloquies, and in ways he may not have been aware, Hitler himself spoke in the very words of Christ and the scriptures — thereby revealing a considerable knowledge of the Bible. A few examples will suffice here: in dedicating the House of German Art in Munich he observed, "Man does not live by bread alone." In talking to the Brownshirts on January 30, 1936, he echoed the words of Jesus to his disciples as recorded in St. John's Gospel, saying, "I have come to know thee. Who thou art, thou art through me, and all I am, I am through thee." He reminded one of his disciples that "I have not come to Germany to bring peace but a sword." In a public speech in Graz in 1938 he announced, "God Almighty has created the Nation. And what the Lord has joined together let not Man set asunder."

He was particularly prone to Biblical quotations when talking to the Hitler Youth. On September 5, 1934, he told them, "You are flesh of our flesh and blood of our blood." In 1932 he advised them either to be "hot or cold, but the lukewarm should be damned and spewed from your mouth." The phrasing is too close to the New Testament to be coincidental. The Revelation of St. John reads: "I know thy works, that thou art neither cold nor hot; I would thou wert cold or hot. So then, because thou art lukewarm, and neither cold nor hot, I will spew thee out of my mouth."

During one of the last suppers with his followers, Hitler invited them to eat of their leader's body, asking them if they would like some blood sausage made from his own blood. In effect he was saying, "Take, eat: this is my body, which is broken for you. . . . "

The defense mechanism used by Adolf Hitler that had the greatest historical consequence was that of projection. Hitler made his own feelings of guilt more bearable by shifting the finger of guilt away from himself and pointing it at Jews. Allport has given a succinct description of the process and has shown the connection between guilt and self-hatred with the need for projection:

> *The hated scapegoat is merely a disguise for persistent and unrecognized self-hatred. A vicious circle is established. The more the sufferer hates himself, the more he hates the scapegoat, the less sure he is of his . . . innocence; hence the more guilt he has to project.*

It needs to be emphasized that in Hitler's case both the degree of self-hatred and the corresponding amount of projected hatred were of truly monumental proportions. He hated Jews for many reasons and accused them of every conceivable crime. But never did he become "so emotional, so arbitrary and so absurd" as when he fulminated against Jewish sex crimes, incest, and perversion — precisely those sexual aberrations about which he felt personally so guilty. The direct projection onto the Jews of guilt felt as the result of his own perversions is shown in an incident in 1938 involving the dismissal of General Werner von

Blomberg as minister of defense. Hitler expressed outraged shock at the disclosure that the general had married a former prostitute. He used the scandal as an excuse for dismissing an uncooperative general, and had the Gestapo collect incriminating evidence against Frau General Blomberg. They supplied him with photographs which showed her plying her profession by participating in various forms of deviant sexual activity. A man who has seen the photographs says that they were of "the most shocking depravity." What concerns us here is Hitler's instinctive reaction upon first seeing the pictures. He said at once that the male partner in the photographs "*must have been* of Jewish extraction." He then became "absolutely convulsed by the wildest anti-Semitic outpouring he had ever given vent to in his entire life."

Thus did the Jews become the hated personal enemy of Hitler and his Reich. In destroying the Jewish people, Adolf Hitler was not only "doing the work of the Lord." He was destroying the evil thing which he felt within himself. This would seem to be the meaning of the curious comment he once made to Rauschning: "The Jew is always within us" [*Der Jude sitzt immer in uns*].

The historical importance of this projection is clear: the racial anti-Semitism which lay at the very core of German fascism and which produced the greatest mass horror of history was, among other things, a direct consequence of Adolf Hitler's personal feelings of guilt and self-hatred.

Peter Loewenberg

The Appeal To Youth

The historical relationship between the events of World War I and its catastrophic aftermath in Central Europe and the rise of National Socialism has often been postulated. The causal relationship is usually drawn from the savagery of trench warfare on the western front, the

From Peter Loewenberg, "The Psychohistorical Origins of the Nazi Youth Cohort," from *American Historical Review* 76, no. 5 (December 1971). Copyright Peter Loewenberg, 1971. Reprinted by permission of the author.

bitterness of defeat and revolution, to the spectacular series of National Socialist electoral victories beginning in 1930, as if such a relationship were historically self-evident. It is the thesis of this paper that the relationship between the period from 1914 to 1920 and the rise and triumph of National Socialism from 1929 to 1935 is specifically generational. The war and postwar experiences of the small children and youth of World War I explicitly conditioned the nature and success of National Socialism. The new adults who became politically effective after 1929 and who filled the ranks of the SA and other paramilitary party organizations such as the Hitler-Jugend and the Bund-Deutscher-Mädel were the children socialized in the First World War.

This essay examines what happened to the members of this generation in their decisive period of character development — particularly in early childhood — and studies their common experiences in childhood, in psychosexual development, and in political socialization that led to similar fixations and distortions of adult character. The specific factors that conditioned this generation include the prolonged absence of the parents, the return of the father in defeat, extreme hunger and privation, and a national defeat in war, which meant the loss of the prevailing political authority and left no viable replacement with which to identify.

Most explanations for the rise of National Socialism stress elements of continuity in German history. These explanations point to political, intellectual, social, diplomatic, military, and economic factors, all of which are important and none of which should be ignored. The historian and social scientist studying Nazism should be conversant with and well versed in these categories of explanation. The study of political leadership is also of unquestioned importance for the understanding of the dynamics of totalitarianism, and it should be intensively developed by historians as an approach to that understanding.

This essay, however, will focus not on the leader but on the followers, not on the charismatic figure but rather on the masses who endow him with special superhuman qualities. It will apply psychoanalytic perceptions to the problem of National Socialism in German history in order to consider the issues of change rather than continuity in history, to deal with social groups rather than individual biography, and to focus on the ego-psychological processes of adaptation to the historical, political, and socioeconomic context rather than on the instinctual biological drives that all men share.

The rapid political ascendancy of the NSDAP in the period from 1928 to 1933 was marked by particularly strong support from youth. Since this generation experienced childhood deprivation in World War I, the argument becomes a psychoanalytical one of taking seriously the developments of infancy and childhood and their effect on behavior in adulthood. I wish to offer an added factor, one to be included as an explanation in addition to rather than instead of the other explanatory schemata of history. Both history and psychoanalysis subscribe to over-determination in causation. It would be a poor historian who sought to attribute a war or a revolution to only a single cause. Similarly in psychoanalytic theory every symptom and symbol is psychically over-determined and serves multiple functions. When the subject of study is a modern totalitarian mass movement it requires analysis utilizing all the tools for perceiving and conceptualizing irrational and affective behavior that the twentieth century has to offer, including psychoanalysis and dynamic psychology.

No genuine historical understanding is possible without the perspective of self-understanding from which the historian can then move forth to deal with historical materials. Likewise there can be no measure of historical understanding if we research what men said and did and fail to understand why they acted. The twentieth century has experienced the gross magnification of political and personal irrationality correlative to the exponential increment in the power of modern technology. No history will speak with relevance or accuracy to the contemporary human condition if it fails to assess realistically the profound capacity of the irrational to move men. . . .

Rather than proceeding with the story of the Nazi youth cohort chronologically and beginning with its origins, this essay will use what Marc Bloch termed the "prudently retrogressive" method of looking at the outcome first, and then tracking down the beginnings or "causes" of the phenomenon. This, of course, corresponds to the clinical method of examining the "presenting complaints" first and then investigating etiology. The outcome of the story in this case is the related and concomitant economic depression, the influx of German youth to the ranks of National Socialism, the political decline of the Weimar Republic, and the Nazi seizure of power.

The Great Depression hit Germany harder than any other country, with the possible exception of the United States. Germany's gross national income, which rose by 25 percent between 1925 and 1928, sank

43 percent from 71 billion RM in 1929 to 41 billion RM in 1932. The production index for industry in 1927–1928 was halved by 1932–1933. In the critical area of capital goods, production in 1933 was one-third of what it had been five years earlier. The very aspect of Nazi success at the polls in the elections of 1930 accelerated the withdrawal of foreign capital from Germany, thus deepening the financial crisis.

The greatest social impact of the economic crisis was in creating unemployment. By 1932 one of every three Germans in the labor market was without a job. This meant that even those who held jobs were insecure, for there were numerous workers available to take the place of every employee. The young people were, of course, the most vulnerable sector of the labor market. New jobs were nonexistent, and the young had the least seniority and experience with which to compete for employment. To this must be added that the number of apprenticeships was sharply diminishing for working-class youths. For example, apprenticeships in iron, steel, and metalworking declined from 132,000 in 1925 to 19,000 in 1932. University graduates had no better prospects for finding employment. They soon formed an underemployed intellectual proletariat that looked to National Socialism for relief and status.

The electoral ascendancy of the Nazi party in the four years between 1928 and 1932 constitutes one of the most dramatic increments of votes and political power in the history of electoral democracy. In the Reichstag elections of May 20, 1928, the National Socialists received 810,127 votes, constituting 2.6 percent of the total vote and 12 Reichstag seats. In the communal elections of 1929 the Nazis made decisive gains. With this election Germany had its first Nazi minister in Thuringia in the person of Wilhelm Frick, a putschist of 1923. In the next Reichstag elections of September 14, 1930, the National Socialists obtained 6,379,672 votes, for 18.3 percent of the total and 107 seats. At the election of July 31, 1932, the National Socialists became the largest party in the country and in the Reichstag with 13,765,781 votes, giving them 37.4 percent of the total vote and 230 parliamentary seats.

This extremely rapid growth of Nazi power can be attributed to the participation in politics of previously inactive people and of those who were newly enfranchised because they had reached voting eligibility at 20 years of age. There were 5.7 million new voters in 1930. The participation of eligible voters in elections increased from 74.6 percent in 1928 to 81.41 percent in 1930, and 83.9 percent in 1932. In the elections of March 5, 1933, there were 2.5 million new voters over the previous year and voting participation rose to 88.04 percent of the electorate.

The German political sociologist, Heinrich Streifler, makes the point that not only were new, youthful voters added at each election, but there were losses from the voting rolls due to deaths that must be calculated. He shows that 3 million voters died in the period between 1928 and 1933. The increment of first-time, new voters in the same period was 6.5 million.

In the elections of 1928, 3.5 million young voters who were eligible did not participate in the voting. "This," says Streifler, "is a reserve that could be mobilized to a much greater extent than the older nonvoters." He goes on to suggest that these young nonvoters were more likely to be mobilized by a radical party that appealed to passions and emotions than to reason.

The Nazis made a spectacular and highly successful appeal to German youth. An official slogan of the party ran "National Socialism is the organized will of youth" (*Nationalsozialismus ist organisierter Jugendwille*). Nazi propagandists like Gregor Strasser skillfully utilized the theme of the battle of the generations. "Step down, you old ones!" (*Macht Platz, ihr Alten!*) he shouted as he invoked the names of the senior political leaders from Left to Right and associated them with the disappointments of the generation of the fathers and the deprivations of war, defeat, and revolution.

> *Whether they are named Scheidemann and Wels, whether Dernberg or Koch, whether Bell and Marx, Stresemann and Riesser, whether Hergt and Westarp — they are the same men we know from the time before the war, when they failed to recognize the essentials of life for the German people; we know them from the war years, when they failed in the will to leadership and victory; we know them from the years of revolution, when they failed in character as well as in ability, in the need of an heroic hour, which, if it had found great men, would have been a great hour for the German people — who, however, became small and mean because its leading men were small and mean.*

The Nazis developed a strong following among the students, making headway in the universities in advance of their general electoral successes. National Socialism made its first visible breakthrough into a mass sector of the German people with its conquest of academic youth. The student government (ASTA) elections of 1929 were called a "National Socialist storm of the universities" by the alarmed opposition press. The Nazi Student Organization (Nationalsozialistische Deutsche Studentenbund) received more than half the votes and dominated the student government in 1929 at the universities of Erlangen and Greifswald. In the 1930 student election it also captured absolute majorities in the universities of Breslau, Giessen, Rostock, Jena, Königsberg, and the Berlin Technische Hochscule. Both of these student elections preceded the Reichstag elections of 1930 in which the Nazis made their decisive breakthrough into the center of national political life. Developments toward National Socialism among the university students anticipated by four years the developments in German society at large.

The comparative age structure of the Nazi movement also tells a story of youthful preponderance on the extreme Right. According to the Reich's census of 1933, those 18 to 30 constituted 31.1 percent of the German population. The proportion of National Socialist party members of this age group rose from 37.6 percent in 1931 to 42.2 percent a year later, on the eve of power. "The National Socialist party," says the sociologist Hans Gerth, "could truthfully boast of being a 'young party.' " By contrast, the Social Democratic party, second in size and the strongest democratic force in German politics, had only 19.3 percent of its members in the 18 to 30 age group in 1931. In 1930 the Social Democrats reported that less than 8 percent of their membership was under 25, and less than half was under 40.

"National Socialism," says Walter Laqueur, the historian of the German youth movement, "came to power as the party of youth." The Nazi party's ideology and organization coincided with those of the elitist and antidemocratic elements of the German youth movement. The Wandervogel, while essentially nonpolitical, retreated to a rustic life on the moors, heaths, and forests where they cultivated the bonds of group life. The Nazi emphasis on a mystical union of blood and soil, of *Volk*, nation, language, and culture, appealed to the romanticism of German youth *Bünde*.

The Hitler Youth adopted many of the symbols and much of the content of the German youth movement. The Nazis incorporated the uniform, the Führer principle and authoritarian organization (group, tribe, *gau*), the flags and banners, the songs, and the war games of the *Bünde*. The National Socialists were able to take over the youth movement with virtually no opposition. On April 15, 1933, the executive of the Grossdeutsche Jugendbund voted to integrate with the Nazi movement. On June 17, 1933, the Jugendbund was dissolved and Baldur von Schirach was appointed the supreme youth leader by Hitler.

A number of scholars have interpreted the radicalization of newly enfranchised German youth in the years of the rise of National Socialism. The Nazification of the youth has also been variously attributed to the spirit of adventure and idealism, a lust for violence and military discipline, the appeal of an attack on age and established power, and the quest for emotional and material security. . . .

There is ample evidence that this generation of German youth was more inclined toward violent and aggressive, or what psychoanalysts call "acting-out," behavior than previous generations. At this point the explanations offered for this phenomenon are inadequate in their one-dimensionality. To say that the youth craved action or that they sought comfort in the immersion in a sheltering group is to beg the question of what made this generation of German youth different from all previous generations. What unique experiences did this group of people have in their developmental years that could induce regression to infantile attitudes in adulthood? One persuasive answer lies in fusing the knowledge we have of personality functioning from psychoanalysis — the most comprehensive and dynamic theory of personality available to the social and humanistic sciences today — with the cohort theory of generational change from historical demography and with the data on the leadership and structure of the Nazi party that we have from the researches of political scientists, historians, and sociologists.

In the half century prior to World War I Germany was transformed from an agricultural to an industrial economy, and her population grew from an agriculturally self-sufficient 40 million to 77 million by 1913. This mounting industrial population made her increasingly dependent on the importation of foreign foodstuffs. In the decade preceding World War I, five-sixths of Germany's vegetable fats, more than half of her dairy goods, and one-third of the eggs her people consumed were imported. This inability to be self-sufficient in foodstuffs made the German population particularly susceptible to the weapon of the blockade. The civilian population began to feel the pressure of severe shortages in 1916. The winter of 1916–1917 is still known as the infamous "turnip winter," in which hunger and privation became widespread experiences in Germany. Getting something to eat was the foremost concern of most people. The official food rations for the summer of 1917 were

1,000 calories per day, whereas the health ministry estimated that 2,280 calories was a subsistence minimum. From 1914 to 1918 three-quarters of a million people died of starvation in Germany.

The armistice of November 11,1918, did not bring the relief that the weary and hungry Germans anticipated. The ordeal of the previous three years was intensified into famine in the winter of 1918–1919. The blockade was continued until the Germans turned over their merchant fleet to the Allies. The armistice blockade was extended by the victorious Allies to include the Baltic Sea, thus cutting off trade with Scandinavia and the Baltic states. Although the Allies undertook responsibility for the German food supply under Article 26 of the Armistice Agreement, the first food shipment was not unloaded in Hamburg until March 26, 1919. On July 11, 1919, the Allied Supreme Economic Council decided to terminate the blockade of Germany as of the next day, July 12. Unrestricted trade between the United States and Germany was resumed three days later, on July 15.

The degree of German suffering under the postwar Allied blockade is a matter on which contemporary opinions differed. Some Allied diplomats and journalists charged that the German government exaggerated the plight of her people in order to increase Allied food deliveries. Today the weight of the historical evidence is that there was widespread extreme hunger and malnutrition in the last three years of the war, which was intensified by the postwar blockade. We may concur with the evaluation of two American historians that "the suffering of the German children, women, and men, with the exception of farmers and rich hoarders, was greater under the continued blockade than prior to the Armistice."

Among the documents that Matthias Erzberger, the chairman of the German Armistice Commission in 1918, requested from the Reichsgesundheitsamt (Reich's public health service) was a memorandum discussing the effects of the blockade on the civilian population. The memorandum, entitled "Damage to the Strength of the German People due to the Enemy Blockade Which Contravenes International Law," was submitted on December 16, 1918. This document is of special psychological interest because it consists of statistics giving increases in deaths, disease, stillbirths, and loss of strength in the labor force, all of which bear sums indicating monetary losses per individual and to the nation. The most remarkable set of figures are those that conclude that, on the basis of a population of 50 million with an average weight of 114.4 pounds, who have each lost one-fifth of their weight, the German people have lost 520,000 tons of human mass (*Menschenmasssse*). The memorandum goes on to estimate that 1.56 million to 1,768,000 tons of food would be necessary to restore the flesh (*Fleische*) that had been lost according to the previous calculation.

The demographic and statistical data constitute an overwhelming case that the German civil population, particularly infants and children, suffered widely and intensively during the war and blockade. Public health authorities and medical researchers have compiled population studies indicating damage to health, fertility, and emotions from 1914 to 1920. These are quantifiable indexes of physical deprivation from which the equally damaging but much more difficult to measure facts of emotional deprivation may be inferred.

On the grossest level the figures show a decline in the number of live births from 1,353,714 in 1915 to 926,813 in 1918. The birth rate per 1,000 population, including stillbirths, declined from 28.25 in 1913 to 14.73 in 1918. The number of deaths among the civilian population over one year old rose from 729,000 in 1914 to 1,084,000 in 1918. While there was a decline in deaths from causes related to nutrition and caloric intake, such as diabetes mellitus, alcoholism, obesity, diseases of the gastrointestinal tract, as well as a decrease in suicides, the gross mortality of the German population increased due to malnutrition, lack of heating, and consequent weakened resistance to disease. Specific causes of death that increased sharply during the war were influenza, lung infections and pneumonia, tuberculosis, diseases of the circulatory system, diphtheria, typhus, dysentery, and diseases of the urinary and reproductive organs. All these diseases indicate a population whose biological ability to maintain health and to counter infection had been seriously undermined in the war years.

Upon looking at the comparative statistics for neonates and infants, we find a decline in weight and size at birth, a decline in the ability of mothers to nurse, a higher incidence of disease, particularly rickets and tuberculosis, as well as an increase in neurotic symptoms such as bedwetting and an increment in the death rate. In the third year of the war the weight of neonates was 50 to 100 grams less at birth than before the war. In one Munich clinic in the year 1918 the females averaged 50 grams and the males 70 grams less at birth than in peacetime.

During the first year of the war more mothers nursed babies and the period of breast feeding was longer than previously, but by the winter of

1915 a decline in breast feeding had set in that was to continue through 1919. This is attributed to the war work of mothers and the "prolonged malnutrition and the damaged body of the mother due to psychic insult." One chemical analysis done in Berlin found a marked decline in the quantity and quality of mother's milk resulting in the retarded development of breast-fed children and a delay in their normal weight gain. Infants fed on cow's milk also received milk that was short of nutriments, butterfat, and vitamins because of the lack of feed for the milk cows and the skimming off of cream for butter production. To the shortage and inferior quality of milk must be added the almost total absence of fresh vegetables and fruit, important sources of vitamins, in the diets of children during the war and postwar period. . . .

World War I was the first total war in history — it involved the labor and the commitment of full energies of its participant peoples as no previous war had. The men were in the armed services, but a modern war requires a major industrial plant and increased production of foodstuffs and supplies to support the armies. Yet the number of men working in industry in Germany dropped 24 percent between 1913 to 1917. In the state of Prussia in 1917 the number of men working in plants employing over ten workers was 2,558,000, including foreigners and prisoners of war, while in 1913 the total of men employed had been 3,387,000.

In Germany this meant a shift of major proportions of women from the home and domestic occupations to war work. In the state of Prussia alone the number of women engaged in industrial labor rose by 76 percent, from 788,100 in 1913 to 1,393,000 in 1917. For Germany as a whole 1.2 million women newly joined the labor force in medium- and large-sized plants during the war. The number of women workers in the armaments industry rose from 113,750 in 1913 to 702,100 in 1917, a gain of 500 percent. The number of women laborers who were covered under compulsory insurance laws on October 1, 1917, was 6,750,000. The increase of adult female workers in Prussia in 1917 was 80.4 percent over 1913. The number of women railroad workers in Prussia rose from 10,000 in 1914 to 100,000 in 1918, an increase of 1,000 percent.

Another new factor in the labor force was the youthful workers. The number of adolescents aged 14 to 16 employed in chemical manufacturing increased 225 percent between 1913 and 1917. For heavy industry the corresponding figure was 97 percent. Many of these were young girls aged 16 to 21. This age group constituted 29 percent of all working women.

That German women were massively engaged in war work was recognized as having resulted in the neglect of Germany's war children and damage to the health of the mothers. Reports came from government offices of increased injuries to children of ages 1 to 5 years due to lack of supervision. S. Rudolf Steinmetz evaluates the demoralization of youth between 1914 and 1918 as an indirect consequence of the war. He ascribes to "the absence of many fathers, the war work of many mothers" the damaged morals and morality of youth.

Many of the war-related phenomena under discussion were not unique to the Central European countries. The factor of a chauvinistic atmosphere of war propaganda was certainly present in all belligerent countries. The absence of the parents in wartime service was also not unique to Germany or Austria. The children of other countries involved in the war too had absent parents and were often orphaned. French and British families undoubtedly experienced the sense of fatherlessness and desertion by the mother as much as did German and Austrian families. Two added factors, however, make the critical difference in the constellation of the child's view of the world: the absence of German and Austrian parents was coupled with extreme and persistent hunger bordering in the cities on starvation, and when the German or Austrian father returned he came in defeat and was unable to protect his family in the postwar period of unemployment and inflation. Not only was the nation defeated, but the whole political-social world was overturned. The kaiser of Germany had fled, and the kaiser of Austria had been deposed. Some Germans would say that the kaiser had deserted his people, to be replaced by an insecure and highly ambivalent republic under equivocating socialist leadership. Much more than an army collapsed — an entire orientation to the state and the conduct of civic life was under assault in 1918–1919. These national factors unique to Central Europe exacerbated the familial crisis of the absence of parents and made of this wartime experience a generational crisis. . . .

When a child who is struggling with his aggressive and destructive impulses finds himself in a society at war, the hatred and violence around him in the outer world meet the as yet untamed aggression raging in his inner world. At the very age when education is beginning to deal with the impulses in the inner environment the same wishes receive sanction and validation from a society at war. It is impossible to repress murderous and destructive wishes when fantasied and actual fighting, maiming, and killing are the preoccupation of all the people among whom the child lives. Instead of turning away from the horrors and atrocities of war, he turns toward them with primitive excitement. The very murderous and destructive impulses that he has been trying to bury in himself are now nourished by the official ideology and mass media of a country at war.

The power of his aroused inner fantasies of violence is anxiety-producing for the child. It is as though an inner signal alerts him to beware of the danger of losing control. When, in addition, the child is not with his family, he will often develop the symptoms of nervousness, bed-wetting, fecal incontinence, stealing, truancy, and delinquency that Winnicott describes.

Many political scientists and historians have pointed to the function of National Socialism as a defense against emotional insecurity. Harold Lasswell, in contrast to those who have interpreted Hitler as a father or a son symbol, develops precisely the theme of Hitler's maternal function for the German people, suggesting that Nazism was a regressive attempt to compensate for mothering and family life that had been inadequate. Lasswell stresses the imagery of cleanliness and pollution of the anal phase.

> *There is a profound sense in which Hitler himself plays a maternal role for certain classes in German society. His incessant moralizing is that of the anxious mother who is totally preoccupied with the physical, intellectual and ethical development of her children. He discourses in public, as he has written in his autobiography, on all manner of pedagogical problems, from the best form of history teaching to the ways of reducing the ravages of social disease. His constant preoccupation with "purity" is consistent with these interests; he alludes constantly to the "purity of the racial stock" and often to the code of personal abstinence or moderation. This master of modern Galahadism uses the language of Protestant puritanism and of Catholic reverence for the institution of family life. The conscience for which he stands is full of obsessional doubts, repetitive affirmations, resounding negations and stern compulsions. It is essentially the bundle of "don'ts" of the nursemaid conscience.*

Similarly, research indicates that paternal deprivation in childhood, which assumes increasing importance in later years as the child approaches and works through his Oedipal conflict, also has a profound impact on the personality and ideas of youth concerning father images,

The Idol of the People. Shown here signing autographs at the 1936 Olympic Games, Hitler apparently saw no contradiction between his image as a father figure to the entire German population and the ruthless brutality with which he crushed opposition to his acquisition of power. (UPI/Bettmann Newsphotos)

political authority, and sources of power. In a study comparing father-separated from father-at-home elementary school children, George R. Bach found that "father separated children produce an idealistic fantasy picture of the father" that "seems[s] to indicate the existence of strong drives for paternal affection." In turn, then, "the severely deprivated [sic] drive for paternal affection provides strong instigation for the idealistic, wish-fulfilling fantasies." The absent father is idealized. This is in part a reaction formation — that is, a defense against hatred toward the father by replacing these repressed hostile feelings with their conscious opposite.

Psychoanalytic theory and clinical evidence tell us that prolonged absence of the father results in intensified closeness to the mother. This in turn will heighten Oedipal conflict for the son in latency. Stimulated incestuous fantasies will increase the fear of punishment for the forbidden longings. The sharpened castration anxiety of the boy left alone with his mother results in strengthened identification with the absent idealized father and in homosexual longings for him. The homosexual feelings for the distant father are a love for him shared with the mother and a defense against heightened incestuous feelings for her.

The emancipation of women, which was accelerated greatly in World War I by the needs of a total war economy, gave to women what had been traditionally men's vocational roles and familial responsibilities. In such circumstances, in her own eyes and in the eyes of her children, the woman who works in industry and agriculture is now doing "man's" work. Thus the mother who manages the affairs of the family may acquire a "phallic" or masculine image to her children. As she is not accustomed to bearing the full responsibility for the family welfare and discipline, she might tend to become anxious. This anxiety is further exacerbated by her sexual and emotional frustration and concern for her husband. Anxieties of all kinds are immediately and inevitably communicated to children, who then become anxious as well. In her uncertainty a mother will often be more punitive than she would be under normal circumstances, both to ward off her own sexual feelings and because of anxiety about her role as disciplinarian. This heightens the passive masochism and castration anxiety in young boys.

Boys who become homosexuals are often those who were left alone with their mothers and formed an intense attachment to them that was unmediated by the father's presence and protection. The struggle against feminine identification and the regression to narcissistic object choice — that is, choosing someone who is like himself, what he was, or what he would like to be — are all generally intensified in boys raised without fathers. . . .

We must seek the widest possible type and range of clinical material, cultural documentation, and quantitative statistical data in our quest for historical evidence. This essay will present three bodies of historical materials, some from each of these categories of data: comparative, qualitative, and quantitative. All varieties of historical evidence have an important and complementary function in generating new hypotheses, contributing new insight, and demarking future areas of exploration. . . .

A study such as the present one, which attempts to assess the impact on children of a catastrophe like a war, should use the best clinical observations in comparative historical situations when these are available. If wartime deprivation has profound emotional effects on young children, these effects should not be limited to one time and place in the modern world. The findings in Germany should also be evident in another industrial land and for other twentieth-century wars, such as for England in World War II.

The British experience is especially valuable to the historian who would consider the emotional effect of war on children because many English children were evacuated from their homes and families in London and the other big cities during World War II, and they were helped through this trying experience by the expert guidance of such specialists in the psychology of children as Anna Freud, Dorothy T. Burlingham, and D. W. Winnicott. These psychoanalysts carried out close residential observation of the evacuated children and published detailed studies of the children's responses and adaptations to the breakup of families in wartime. These were "normal" children, they were not hospitalized, nor were they juvenile offenders. They were not so heavily traumatized by their experience that their regressive defenses resisted all modification, as is the case with most of the children who survived concentration camps. The blitzed English children were provided with a homelike environment and encouraged in every way toward normal development. The fact that they were out of their homes and away from their families provides a degree of objectivity to the observations. The data were not filtered through reports of the parents; they are first-hand observations by trained professionals.

Anna Freud and Burlingham found that while a child will accept mother substitutes in the absence of its own mother, "there is . . . no father substitute who can fill the place which is left empty by the child's own father." "The infant's emotional relationship to its father begins later in life than that of its mother," they write, "but certainly from the second year onward it is an integral part of its emotional life and a necessary ingredient in the complex forces which work towards the formation of its character and its personality."

The researchers found that absent parents were greatly idealized. Their letters were carried around and had to be read to the children innumerable times. When the father was away in the armed services he was spoken of by his child in terms of endearment and admiration. Especially children who were in reality rejected or disappointed by their fathers formed passionate, loving, and admiring relationships to them. When a child had never known his father he would invent an idealized fantasy father who sanctioned his forbidden greedy and destructive wishes, who loved him and gave him security.

When a father came home on leave, however, and thereby encroached on the existing close mother-child relationship, he was met with resentment and hostility by the child. The father was viewed as an intruder who separated the mother and son. One little boy said: "Do write to my Daddy, I don't want him to come here. I don't want to have lunch with him. Somebody else can have my Daddy." But the same son and his father were best of friends when they were left alone without the mother.

When in some cases the ultimate disaster struck, Anna Freud and Burlingham report a complete inability of the children to accept their father's death. All the orphaned children talked about their dead fathers as if they were still alive. They denied the fact of death with fantasies of the father's rebirth and return from heaven.

The most original psychoanalytical approach to National Socialist youth, and the one that I find conceptually most perceptive and useful, is Martin Wangh's excellent analysis of 1964. He structures the psychodynamics of the First World War German children who came to the age of political effectiveness with the rise of Hitler with precision and insight. A preoccupation with guilt, Wangh points out, is also an unrecognized self-reproach for unresolved aggression against the father. Aggression toward the absent father-rival is expressed in gleeful ideas concerning his degradation and defeat. But the hostility is coupled with a longing for the idealized father that exacerbates childish homosexual wishes. Those homosexual longings offer a way out of the Oedipal conflict that is heightened for sons left alone with their mothers. In these circumstances the woman is often rejected, and the incestuous wish is ascribed to someone else. These mental defenses, Wangh suggests, were renewed in the Nazi movement's deification of the Führer and its infernalization of the Jew. Homosexual tension was relieved through submission to an all-powerful leader, through turning women into "breeders" of children, and by persecuting Jews as "incestuous criminals" and "defilers of the race." The passive-masochistic inclinations that develop when boys are brought up and disciplined by mothers who are anxious and punitive may be defended against by preference for submission to a man, as this is less threatening and less castrating than submission to a woman. Self-humiliation and self-contempt were displaced onto the Jews and other supposedly inferior people, thereby assuaging feelings of unworthiness and masochistic fantasies of rejection. Since the former wartime enemies were for the time being unassailable, the Jew, who was defenseless and available, became by the mechanism of displacement the victim of those who needed a target for regressive action. . . .

Among the richest sources for the expression of the experience of young Germans during the war and postwar years is the literature of the period, which more than held its place amid the cultural fecundity of the Weimer epoch. Sometimes literary expression can capture for historians the essence of a generation's experience both graphically and with a depth of emotional subtlety that cannot be conveyed by statistics or quantitative data. Many qualitative affects cannot be statistically comprehended or documented. It is possible to see, identify, and demonstrate father identification and castration anxiety without necessarily being able to computerize them. This is the appeal to the historian of both clinical insight and literary sensibility. Can one measure or compare quantitatively, for example, the degree of suffering, mourning, loss, or rage a subject feels? For this kind of emotional evidence we must rely on that most sensitive of our cultural materials — the subjective written word of literature.

When this has been said, it is nevertheless astonishing to experience the great autobiographical pacifist novel *Jahrgang 1902* by Ernst Glaeser (1902–1963), which describes the author's feelings with such intensity and pathos that it often reads more like the free associations of a patient in psychoanalysis than a novel. The critic William Soskin ranked *Jahrgang 1902* with *Sergeant Grisha* and *All Quiet on the Western Front* as one of the most significant works on the First World War. This book ran through six German printings during the winter of 1928–1929. It sold 70,000 copies in Germany and was translated into twenty-five languages.

The book takes its title from the year of the author's birth, which also automatically became the year of his military-service class. The class of 1902 was not to experience the war of 1914–1918 on the front.[1] For that they were too young, but as Glaeser pointedly noted, "The war did not establish a moratorium on puberty." The book, he said, deals with "the tragedy of murdered minds and souls and diseased temperaments in the noncombatant social body."

As the war began the fathers left to join their regiments and the twelve-year-old boy observes that "life in our town became quieter." The boys played war games in which the French and Russians were always soundly beaten. The fathers were sorely missed. They were quickly idealized and glorified. Glaeser describes the process of overestimation and identification with the father who is absent at war:

> We thought only of our fathers in these days. Overnight they had become heroes. . . . We loved our fathers with a new sublime love. As ideals. And just as we formerly used to express our admiration for the

---

[1] For a sardonic expression from among the youngest class that went to war, see Erich Kästner, "The Class of 1899," in his *Bei Durchsicht meiner Bücher* . . . (Zurich: Atrium Verlag, 1946), 97–98. "We took the women to bed, / While the men stood in France. / We had imagined that it would be much more wonderful. / We were merely confirmants. / Then they took us to the army, / For nothing more than cannon fodder. / The benches at school were emptied, / Mother wept at home. / Then we had a bit of revolution / And potato chips came raining down. / Then came the women, just like they used to / And then we caught the clap. / Meanwhile the old man lost his money, / So we became night-school students / By day we worked in an office / And dealt with rates of interest. / Then she almost had a child. / Whether by you or by me — who knows! / A friend of ours scraped it out. / And the next thing you know we will be thirty. / We even passed an examination / And have already forgotten most of it. / Now we are alone day and night / And have nothing decent to eat! / We looked the world straight in the snout, / Instead of playing with dolls / We spit at the rest of the world, / Insofar as we were not killed at Ypres. / They made our bodies or our spirit / A wee bit too weak / They threw us into world history too long, / Too fast, and too much. / The old folks maintained that the time has come / For us to sow and to reap. / But wait a moment. Soon we will be ready. / Just a moment. Soon we will be there! / Then we will show you what we have learned!"

Homeric heroes or the figures of the Wars of Liberation by token symbols
of clothing such as golden helmets of tin foil or Lützow caps, so we now
also began, but in far greater measure, to turn ourselves symbolically
into the idealized figures of our fathers.

The boys of the village went to the barber to have their hair cut in the close-cropped military style like their fathers.

We had our hair cut. Bare. Smooth. Three millimeters high. For this is
how we had seen it on our fathers as they left for the front. None of them
had hair to part now.

One evening late in September a group of fifteen determined boys
went to the barber. We stood according to height and let the instrument
pass over our heads. As the barber was sweeping up our hair with a
broom an hour later, he said: "Now you look like recruits."

We were proud of this distinction and enthusiastically paid 40
pfennigs each.

By the winter of 1916 the privation of the war began to be felt in the daily lives of the boys. They were always hungry. There was never enough to eat. The steady diet of turnip soup became inedible. City folk bribed and bartered away precious possessions in order to get nourishing food from the farmers. The mother gave Kathinka, the maid, one of her finest blouses so that she would bring back food when she visited her peasant parents. Faithfully Kathinka smuggled butter past the gendarmes in her woolen bloomers. Field gendarmes and controllers appeared on the roads and at the stations to search travelers for contraband foodstuffs. The children developed tactics for deceiving the gendarmes and smuggling forbidden foodstuffs home. One boy would serve as a decoy to draw the gendarme's attention while the other raced home across the fields with a sack of flour or a ham.

This progression within two years from idealism to hunger and the struggle for survival is vividly described by Glaeser.

The winter remained hard until the end. The war began to burst over
the fronts and to strike the people. Hunger destroyed our unity; in the
families children stole each other's rations. . . . Soon the women who
stood in gray lines in front of the shops talked more about the hunger of
their children than of the death of their husbands. The sensations of war
had been altered.

A new front existed. It was held by women. The enemies were the
entente of field gendarmes and uncompromising guards. Every smug-

> *gled pound of butter, every sack of potatoes gleefully secreted by night was celebrated in the families with the same enthusiasm as the victories of the armies two years earlier. . . . It was wonderful and inspiring to outwit the gendarmes and after successfully triumphing to be honored by one's mother as a hero.*

Oedipal longings were heightened for the sons left alone with their mothers during years of war. Starvation led to the mobilization of unconscious wishes for a return to the oral comforts of early mother-child units. Occasionally the prolonged hunger was broken by feasting on an illegally slaughtered pig or a smuggled goose that the father sent home from the eastern front. Then an orgy of feeding took place. Gluttony reigned and undernourished bellies got sick on the rich food. The windows had to be stuffed to keep the neighbors from smelling the meat. The adolescent boy and his mother consumed almost an entire twelve-pound goose in one night. A stolen drumstick for his girlfriend was to her the convincing symbol of love. Glaeser writes, "We scarcely spoke of the war any more, we only spoke of hunger. Our mothers were closer to us than our fathers."

The fathers were not present to shield the sons from maternal seduction. One young adolescent in the novel is seduced by a motherly farmer's wife with the promise of a large ham. But, much as the pangs of his stomach and his mother's pleading letters argued for bringing the ham home, he could not do it. The great succulent ham had become an incestuous object. He had earned it from the farm wife by taking her husband's place. Now he was too guilty and too anxious to permit himself and his family to enjoy it. The pangs of guilt were stronger than the pains of hunger. As if he could "undo" his Oedipal crime, the boy laid the ham on the farm wife's bed and left. He was tearful and depressed, feelings he rationalized as being due to his injured feelings because he was really only a substitute (*Ersatz*) for the husband. He climbed into bed with his boy comrade. In the stillness of the dawn they embraced, keeping each other warm, and he shared his story of seduction and sexual discovery. In this episode we see fully elaborated the heightened Oedipal conflict when the father is absent, the increased guilt and fear of retribution, and finally the rejection of the woman as a sexual object and an exacerbation of adolescent homosexuality arising from the emotional effects of the war.

By the winter of 1917 the fathers had become aliens to their sons. But they were not only unknown men, they were feared and threatening strangers who claimed rights and control over the lives of their sons. They had become distant but powerful figures who could punish and exact a terrible price for disobedience and transgressions. Glaeser recounts his reaction as a fifteen-year-old to a letter from his father on the Russian front in terms of intense castration anxiety. The adolescent boy's Oedipal victory in having displaced his father would now be terribly expiated and revenged by a towering, castrating monster of his guilt-laden fantasies. Glaeser attempts to deny that his father has any legitimate claim to control over him at all. But his father would know where to find him and the inevitable retribution would be inexorable.

> *We were frightened. That was the voice of the front. That was the voice of those men who formerly were once our fathers, who now, however, removed from us for years, were strangers before us, fearsome, huge, overpowering, casting dark shadows, oppressive as a monument. What did they still know of us? They knew where we lived, but they no longer knew what we looked like and thought.*

It is of biographical interest for the thesis of this essay that Glaeser went into emigration from Germany after 1933, living in Prague, Zurich, and Paris. In Zurich in 1939 he wrote a newspaper article condoning Hitler's policies and condemning his fellow émigrés. Within days he received a contract from a Berlin publisher. He returned to Germany and joined the war effort, becoming a war reporter for the Luftwaffe and the editor of the military newspaper, *Adler im Suden.*

Thus, as did so many others of his cohort, Glaeser was two decades later to choose to wear a uniform and to identify with his distant and glorified father. The identification with the father who went out to war served to erase the memory of the feared and hated strange father who came home in defeat. By being a patriot and submitting to authority, the ambivalence of the young boy who gleefully observed his father's humiliating defeat and degradation was denied and expiated. Now he would do obeisance to an idealized but remote leader who was deified and untouchable. . . .

The third variety of data I wish to examine is quantitative. It is a series of autobiographical essays collected in 1934 by Theodore Abel, a sociologist at Columbia University, in an essay contest offering cash prizes for "the best personal life history of an adherent of the Hitler movement."

In reading the essays one is often struck by their didactic quality. Some writers say outright that they are delighted to write down their experiences for the benefit of American researchers at Columbia University. As the essays were solicited by a bulletin at all local headquarters of the NSDAP and by announcements in the party press, and as the writers were not anonymous, one may infer that the writers suspected that party organs would be informed of any criticism and political or personal deviance in the essays. In some cases one senses that a local party functionary may have encouraged the writers to respond to the essay contest. Some contributions bear the NSDAP Abteiling Propaganda stamp. Many tiresomely repeat propaganda slogans about Jewish war profiteering, Red vandalism in the revolution of 1918–1919, and so forth.

All these caveats notwithstanding, these nearly 600 essays constitute a valuable historical source. In the first place it is a contemporary source. No set of interviews of ex-Nazis thirty-seven years later could possibly elicit the same material. The Abel autobiographies may be utilized, not as a statistical sample for generalizations, but as bases for theory building. They will serve as a cognitive prism for drawing attention to necessary variables of political behavior rather than as a monolithic statistical sample that can produce conclusive findings for the population of the Nazi party. They can tell us, however, what excited and stimulated the writers, what preoccupied their fantasies and imaginations, how they viewed themselves, their childhoods and homes, and their enemies. These data can then become referents for further theoretical conceptualization and behavioral model-building, particularly with respect to emotional connotations that are not censored by the writers because they appear to be apolitical and therefore unimportant.

The most striking emotional affect expressed in the Abel autobiographies are the adult memories of intense hunger and privation from childhood. A party member who was a child of the war years recollects, "Sometimes I had to scurry around eight to ten hours — occasionally at night — to procure a few potatoes or a bit of butter. Carrots and beets, previously considered fit only for cattle, came to be table luxuries." Another man's memory is vivid in its sense of abandonment and isolation expressed in language that makes a feeling of maternal deprivation very clear.

> *Hunger was upon us. Bread and potatoes were scarce, while meat and fats were almost non-existent. We were hungry all the time; we had forgotten how it felt to have our stomachs full.*
>
> *All family life was at an end. None of us really knew what it meant — we were left to our own devices. For women had to take the place of their fighting men. They toiled in factories and in offices, as ostlers and as commercial travelers, in all fields of activity previously allotted to men — behind the plow as well as on the omnibus. Thus while we never saw our fathers, we had only glimpses of our mothers in the evening. Even then they could not devote themselves to us because, tired as they were, they had to take care of their household, after their strenuous day at work. So we grew up, amid hunger and privation, with no semblance of decent family life.*

A study of the Abel autobiographies focused on a sample from the birth cohorts 1911 to 1915, who were small children during the war, indicates the presence of the defensive mechanisms of projection, displacement, low frustration tolerance, and the search for an idealized father. For example, the essays of two sisters born in 1913 and 1915, whose father fell in 1915, clearly demonstrate that Hitler served as an idealized father figure for them. Their earliest memories are of their mother crying a great deal and of all the people wearing black. They relate their excitement at first hearing the Führer speak in person at a rally in Kassel in 1931. The sisters were so exhilarated that neither of them could sleep all night. They prayed for the protection of the Führer, and asked forgiveness for ever having doubted him. The sisters began their Nazi party activities by caring for and feeding SA men.

Some of the men in the Abel Collection who lost their fathers early in life and were separated from their mothers especially valued the comradeship of the SA. One such man wrote, "It was wonderful to belong to the bond of comradeship of the SA. Each one stood up for the other." Massive projection of ego-alien impulses is evident in many of the essays. One man says that bejeweled Jewessess tried to seduce him politically with cake. Many of the SA men who engaged in street brawls and violence blamed others, such as the police and the Communists, for instigating the fighting and for persecuting them. One man displays remarkable projection and displacement of his own murderous feelings toward a younger brother when he relates the death of that brother in an unnecessary operation performed by a Jewish doctor. "Since I especially loved my dead brother," he writes, "a grudge arose in me against the doctor, and this not yet comprehensible hatred increased with age to become an antagonism against everything Jewish." . . .

The demographic factors of massive health, nutritional, and material deprivation and parental absence in Central Europe during World War I should lead the historian to apply theoretical and clinical knowledge of the long-term effects of such a deprived childhood on personality. The anticipation of weakened character structure manifested in aggression, defenses of projection and displacement, and inner rage that may be mobilized by a renewed anxiety-inducing trauma in adulthood is validated in the subsequent political conduct of this cohort during the Great Depression when they joined extremist paramilitary and youth organizations and political parties. In view of these two bodies of data for which a psychoanalytic understanding of personality provides the essential linkage, it is postulated that a direct relationship existed between the deprivation German children experienced in World War I and the response of these children and adolescents to the anxieties aroused by the Great Depression of the early 1930s. This relationship is psychodynamic: the war generation had weakened egos and superegos, meaning that the members of this generation turned readily to programs based on facile solutions and violence when they met new frustrations during the depression. They then reverted to earlier phase-specific fixations in their child development marked by rage, sadism, and the defensive idealization of their absent parents, especially the father. These elements made this age cohort particularly susceptible to the appeal of a mass movement utilizing the crudest devices of projection and displacement in its ideology. Above all it prepared the young voters of Germany for submission to a total, charismatic leader.

But fantasy is always in the end less satisfying than mundane reality. Ironically, instead of finding the idealized father they, with Hitler as their leader, plunged Germany and Europe headlong into a series of deprivations many times worse than those of World War I. Thus the repetition was to seek the glory of identification with the absent soldier-father, but like all quests for a fantasied past, it had to fail. Hitler and National Socialism were so much a repetition and fulfillment of the traumatic childhoods of the generation of World War I that the attempt to undo that war and those childhoods was to become a political program. As a result the regressive illusion of Nazism ended in a repetition of misery at the front and starvation at home made worse by destroyed cities, irremediable guilt, and millions of new orphans.

A return to the past is always unreal. To attempt it is the path of certain disaster. There was no glorified father who went to war and who could be recaptured in Hitler. He existed only in fantasy, and he could never be brought back in reality. There are no ideal mothers and fathers; there are only flawed human parents. Therefore, for a World War I generation seeking restitution of a lost childhood there was to be only bitter reality in the form of a psychotic charlatan who skillfully manipulated human needs and left destruction to Germany and Europe. What the youth cohort wanted was a fantasy of warmth, closeness, security, power, and love. What they recreated was a repetition of their own childhoods. They gave to their children and to Europe in greater measure precisely the traumas they had suffered as children and adolescents a quarter of a century earlier.

The Industrial Might of the Third Reich. This 1940 photo shows tanks being built for use in Hitler's *Blitzkrieg*. (UPI/Bettmann Newsphotos).

PART

 Industry,
Church,
and Army

Variety of Opinion

Among the things that set Nazism apart from the Fascist movements of other countries is the fact that Hitler always found obedient instruments to carry out his eccentric radicalism.

Joachim C. Fest

Quite contrary to the widespread impression that Hitler gained power in January 1933 with strong backing from big business, his appointment to the chancellorship came just when relations between his movement and the business community had reached the lowest point.

Henry Ashby Turner, Jr.

When Hitler persuaded the cabinet on 8 February to endorse the proposition that the highest priority in any future recovery programme must be given to rearmament for the next five years, he was in effect preparing the way . . . for a working partnership between heavy industry, army, and party.

William Carr

The papacy and members of the German hierarchy in the pre-war years had at times denounced the cult of racism, of blood and soil. But there were no clarion protests against the anti-Semitic policy of the Nazi rulers then or during the war years.

Ernst Christian Helmreich

105

> *In the Armed Forces, as among the population generally, there were some brave local groups, though there was no extensive or coordinated organization at all.*
>
> Hans-Adolf Jacobsen

In January 1933 Adolf Hitler became the chancellor of Germany. He was not yet the dictator. First he had to gain the allegiance of the people and, above all, of the elites. Once the political machinery, the courts, and the police were firmly in hand, the Nazi party could persuade business, religious, and military leaders to support a national effort to restore law and order, as well as to regain Germany's rightful place among the states of Europe.

Joachim C. Fest *begins with the Nazi political takeover amidst an initial popular euphoria. He identifies what was unique about this German form of fascism. The key, Fest contends, lay in a fanatical sense of morality. It seemed as though the Nazis succeeded because they were able to convert Germany into one huge Boy Scout camp. In this there was a loss of reality as traditional standards of behavior were set aside and replaced by a special mission to fulfill a higher law. The excitement of Nazism thus led to widespread moral confusion.*

Henry Ashby Turner, Jr., *denies that German business moguls were instrumental either in the collapse of the Weimar Republic or in the rise of the Nazi party. In his economic objectives before 1933 Hitler remained deliberately ambiguous and, accordingly, the business community was puzzled. Turner allows that there was some flirtation between them but little more, as Hitler wooed industrial capitalists with vague promises. Hitler's final surge to power was therefore not financed by the leaders of big business, who mostly preferred their fellow elites and felt they had reason to distrust an outsider.*

William Carr *examines Nazi economic policies after 1933. Once in control, Hitler thwarted the German trade-union movement and made open appeals to the business community. He was soon able to negotiate an arrangement by offering tax breaks, wage controls, and lucrative military contracts. The Führer's bid for respectability with business and banking interests was aided by his financial adviser, Hjalmar Schacht. Their partnership survived until 1936, when Hitler dropped his mask and moved to implement a new four-year economic plan that was frankly geared toward total war. Under these circumstances it was appropriate that Schacht was replaced by Hermann Goering. The ambitions of business did not push Germany to war, Carr believes, but they did become part of a Nazi dynamism in which political, economic, and military interests were impossible to disaggregate.*

Ernst Christian Helmreich *discusses one of Hitler's most delicate problems: to gain the cooperation of the Christian churches. Fortunately for Hitler, both German Protestants and Catholics could be counted on to remain staunch patriots. Especially problematic for church leaders, however, was the Nazi persecution of the Jews. Here controversy is focused on (but not restricted to) the muted opposition of the Catholic hierarchy and the Roman papacy. Paradoxically, Helmreich shows, as German fortunes in the war worsened, state pressure on religious organizations was eased. Yet by then there was little that the Catholic clergy could do without a clear condemnation of Nazi racial policies from the Vatican. That was not forthcoming.*

Hans-Adolf Jacobsen *presents a sketch of those army officers who, after acquiescing in Hitler's high command for many years, at last turned against him when the prospect of military victory began to fade. A conspiracy to kill Hitler formed in 1943. Early centered in the German counterespionage (Abwehr) service around Hans Oster, the Resistance eventually came to include many diverse elements, including several distinguished military personalities. After elaborate preparations to topple the Nazi regime, and after a few assassination attempts on Hitler's life had failed, in July 1944 Colonel Claus Schenk von Stauffenberg planted a time bomb under the Führer's table during a military briefing. The collapse of this plot brought dreadful retribution on the conspirators and ended any prospect for what is here called "the Cause." In the end, as a result, the German Resistance could claim nothing, except perhaps to have rescued the honor of some of those who regretted their pact with the devil.*

In these pages we gain a sense of the complexity of the Nazi experience in Germany. It was a political movement of extraordinary energy that effectively combined enthusiasm and terror so as to discourage overt resistance. Many decent Germans no doubt responded at first to the idealism of a new day, only to watch helplessly thereafter as their hopes were perverted beyond recognition or retrieval.

Joachim C. Fest

Enthusiasm and Confusion

The dramatic ceremonial with which Hitler took over the chancellorship, the accompaniment of torchlight parades and mass demonstrations, bore no relationship to the constitutional importance of the event. For, strictly speaking, January 30, 1933, brought nothing more than a change of administrations. Nevertheless, the public sensed that the appointment of Hitler as Chancellor could not be compared with the cabinet reshufflings of former years. Despite all the vaunted intentions of the German Nationalist coalition partners "to keep the frustrated Austrian painter on the leash," the Nazis from the start made ready to seize full power and to apply it in revolutionary ways. All the efforts of Papen and his fellows to play a part in the oratory, the celebrating, or the directing of affairs only gave the impression of breathless running to keep up. Numerical superiority in the cabinet, influence with the President, or in the economy, the army, and the bureaucracy could not conceal the fact that this was their rival's hour.

After January 30 a mass desertion to the Nazi camp began. Once again the axiom was proved that in revolutionary times principles are cheap, and perfidy, calculation, and fear reign supreme. This was true, but not the whole truth. For the massive political turncoatism bespoke not only lack of character and servility. Quite often it represented the spontaneous desire to give up old prejudices, ideologies, and social restrictions and to join with others in making a fresh start. "We were not all opportunists," wrote the poet Gottfried Benn in retrospect, speaking as one of the vast host of people who were carried along by the force of the spreading revolutionary mood. Powerful traditional parties and associations cracked under the propagandistic onslaught; and even before they were forcibly dissolved and banned they left a leaderless following to its own devices. The past — republic, divisiveness, impotence — was over and done with. A rapidly shrinking minority did not succumb to the frenzy. But such holdouts were driven into isolation; they saw themselves excluded from those celebrations of the new sense of community, from those who could reveal in mass oaths in cathedrals of lights, in addresses by the Führer, in mountaintop bonfires and choral singing by hundreds of thousands of voices. Even the first signs of the reign of terror could not mute the rejoicing. The public mind interpreted the terror as an expression of a ruthlessly operating energy for which it had looked all too long in vain.

These concomitants of enthusiasm are what have given Hitler's seizure of power its distressing note. For they undermine all the arguments for its having been a historical accident, the product of intrigues or dark conspiracies. Any attempt to explain the events of those years has always had to face the question of how Nazism could so rapidly and effortlessly have conquered the majority, not just attained power, in an ancient and experienced civilized nation. And how could it have thrown that majority into a peculiarly hysterical state compounded of enthusiasm, credulity, and devotion? How could the political, social, and moral checks and balances, which a country belonging to the "nobility of nations" after all possesses, have so glaringly failed? Before Hitler came to power, an observer described what he considered the inevitable course of events: "Dictatorship, abolition of the parliament, crushing of all intellectual liberties, inflation, terror, civil war; for the opposition could not simply be made to disappear. A general strike would be called. The unions would provide a core for the bitterest kind of resistance; they would be joined by the Reichsbanner and by all those concerned about the future. And if Hitler won over even the Army and met the opposition with cannon — he would find millions of resolute antagonists." But there were no millions of resolute antagonists and consequently no need for a bloody coup. On the other hand, Hitler did not come like a thief in the night. With his histrionic verbosity he revealed, more perhaps than any other politician, what he had been aiming for through all the byways and tactical maneuvers: dictatorship, anti-Semitism, conquest of living space.

Understandably enough, the euphoria of those weeks gave many observers the impression that Germany had rediscovered her true self. Although the Constitution and the rules of the political game as played in the republic remained valid for the time being, they nevertheless seemed curiously obsolete, cast off like an alien shell. And for decades this image — of a nation that seemed to have found itself in exuberantly turning away from the European tradition of rationality and humane progress — determined the interpretation of events. . . .

Without doubt there were unmistakably German features in National Socialism; but they are of a different and more complex kind than those set forth by Vermeil or Shirer. No genealogy of evil, no single explanation, can do justice to the nature of the phenomenon. Nor should we see its seeds only in the obviously dark and ominous elements in the German past. Many naïve attitudes, or at any rate attitudes that for generations caused no trouble, and even some virtues and commendable values, made the success of Nazism possible. One of the lessons the era has to teach us is that a totalitarian power system need not be built up upon a nation's deviant or even criminal tendencies. A nation cannot decide, like a Richard III, to become a villain. Historical, psychological, and even social conditions comparable to those in Germany existed in many countries, and frequently only a fine line separated other nations from Fascist rule. The Germans were not the only people to arrive late at the sense of nationhood, or to be behindhand at developing democratic institutions. As for the unbridgeable gulfs between liberal and socialist forces, between the bourgeoisie and the working class, these, too, were not peculiarly German. We may also question whether revanchist yearnings, bellicose ideologies, or dreams of great power status were more pronounced in Germany than in some of her European neighbors. And even anti-Semitism, decisively though it governed Hitler's thinking, was surely not a specifically German phenomenon. In fact, it was rather weaker among the Germans than in most other peoples. Racial emotions did not, at any rate, win the masses over to National Socialism or kindle their enthusiasm. Hitler himself was cognizant of this, as his efforts to play down his anti-Semitism during the final phase of his struggle for power plainly showed.

During the same era many Fascist or Fascist-oriented movements came in power — in Italy, Turkey, Poland, Austria, and Spain, for example. What was peculiarly German about National Socialism emerges most clearly by comparison with the systems in these other countries: it was the most radical, the most absolute manifestation of Fascism.

This fundamental rigor, which came out on the intellectual as well as the administrative plane, was Hitler's personal contribution to the nature of National Socialism. In his way of sharply opposing an idea to reality, of elevating what ought to be above what is, he was truly German. The failed local politician, subletting a room on Thierschstrasse, sketched triumphal arches and domed halls that were to assure his posthumous fame. Ignoring mockery, the Chancellor did not reckon in generations, but in millennia; he wanted to undo not merely the Treaty of Versailles and Germany's impotence but nothing less than the consequences of the great migrations. Whereas Mussolini's ambition aimed at restoring a lost historical grandeur, whereas Maurras called for a return to the *ancien régime* and the *"gloire de la Déesse France,"* whereas all the other Fascisms could do no better than invoke a past golden age, Hitler set himself a goal more grandiose than anything the world had ever seen: an empire stretching from the Atlantic to the Urals and from Narvik to Suez. His pure master race seeking its rightful place would fight for and win this empire. Would other countries oppose him? He would crush them. Were peoples located contrary to his plans? He would resettle them. Did the races fail to correspond to his image? He would select, breed, eliminate until the reality fitted his conception. He was always thinking the unthinkable; in his statements an element of bitter refusal to submit to reality invariably emerged. His personality was not without manic characteristics. "I confront everything with a tremendous, ice-cold lack of bias," he declared. He seemed authentically himself only when he spoke and acted with the utmost radicality. To that extent, National Socialism cannot be conceived apart from Hitler.

Among the things that set Nazism apart from the Fascist movements of other countries is the fact that Hitler always found obedient instruments to carry out his eccentric radicalism. No stirrings of pity mitigated the concentrated and punctilious harshness of the regime. Its barbarous features have often been ascribed to the deliberate application of cruelty by murderers and sadists, and such criminal elements continue to loom large in the popular mind. To this day types of this sort appear in literary works, whip in hand, as the personifications of Nazism. But the regime had quite another picture of itself. No question about its making use of such people, especially in the initial phase; but it quickly realized that lasting rule cannot be founded upon the unleashing of criminal instincts. The radicality that constituted the true nature of National Socialism does not really spring from the license it offered to instinctual gratification. The problem was not one of criminal impulses but of a perverted moral energy.

Those to whom Nazism chiefly appealed were people with a strong but directionless craving for morality. In the SS, National Socialism trained this type and organized it into an elite corps. The "inner values" that were perpetually being preached within this secular monastic order — the theme of many an evening meeting complete with romantic torchlight — included, according to the prescript of Heinrich Himmler, the following virtues: loyalty, honesty, obedience, hardness, decency, poverty, and bravery. But all these virtues were detached from any comprehensive frame of reference and directed entirely toward the purposes of the regime. Under the command of such imperatives a type of person was trained who demanded "cold, in fact, stony attitudes" of himself, as one of them wrote, and had "ceased to have human feelings." Out of his harshness toward himself he derived the justification for harshness toward others. The ability to walk over dead bodies was literally demanded of him; and before that could be developed, his own self had to be deadened. It is this impassive, mechanical quality that strikes the observer as far more extreme than sheer brutality. For the killer who acts out of an overpowering social, intellectual, or human resentment exerts a claim, however small, upon our sympathy.

The moral imperative was supplemented and crowned by the idea of a special mission: the sense of taking part in an apocalyptic confrontation, of obeying a "higher law," of being the agent of an ideal. Images and slogans alike were made to seem like metaphysical commandments, and a special consecration was conferred upon relentlessness. That is how Hitler meant it when he denounced those who cast doubt on his mission as "enemies of the people." This fanaticism, this fixation upon his own deeper insight and his own loftier missionary aims, reflected the traditional German false relationship to politics, and beyond that the nation's peculiarly distorted relationship to reality in general. The real world in which ideas take form and are experienced by people, in which thoughts can be translated into despairs, anxieties, hatreds, and terrors, simply did not exist. All that existed was the program, and the process of putting it across, as Hitler occasionally remarked, involved either positive or negative activity. The lack of humanitarian imagination (which comes to the fore whenever Nazi criminals are brought to trial, from the Nuremberg Trials on) was nothing but the expression of this loss of a sense of reality. That was the characteristically German element in National Socialism, and there is reason to believe that various connecting lines run far back into German history.

Henry Ashby Turner, Jr.

The Legend of
Capitalist Support

Only through gross distortion can big business be accorded a crucial, or even major, role in the downfall of the Republic. The business community displayed, to be sure, little enthusiasm for the new democratic state, and very few major executives could be termed democrats by conviction. Particularly at the outset of the republican period they felt jeopardized by a political system that assigned ultimate authority over national policy to a mass electorate. They also deplored many republican policies, especially the rapid expansion of *Sozialpolitik* — welfare state legislation — and direct governmental intervention in labor-management relations. But once the difficulties of the Republic's first five years had been overcome and a measure of prosperity restored, most men of big business reconciled themselves to the new state, if not always to its policies. So long as the country prospered, they saw little chance for a change of regime. Most remained frustrated politically, having discovered that economic potency did not translate readily into political effectiveness in a democratic polity, where ballots weighed more than money and where blocs of disciplined interest-group voters counted for more than did financial contributions.

Big businessmen did, to be sure, play a part in causing the crisis that eventuated in the paralysis of the Republic's parliamentary system in 1930. The insistence by some sectors of big business on curtailment of the capstone of republican *Sozialpolitik*, the national unemployment insurance program, helped at that time to precipitate what in retrospect emerges as one of the earliest of the now familiar fiscal crises of twentieth-century capitalist welfare states. The outcome of that crisis was, however, determined not by the business community but rather by the political spokesmen of organized labor. Also, the resulting parliamentary deadlock did not in itself put an end to Weimar democracy. That stalemate assumed fateful proportions only because it triggered a fundamental shift of authority to the presidency through use of the emergency powers assigned to that office by the constitution. Behind that move stood not Germany's capitalists but rather its military leadership. Generals, not corporation executives, effected the establishment of presidential rule in 1930. As a consequence of that development — which initially made some of the leading figures in the business community very uneasy because of their concern about the reaction of credit markets abroad — they and their compeers found themselves with even less political influence than they had enjoyed earlier. As long as the parliamentary system functioned, the politically active elements of big business had frequently managed to combine their small parliamentary bloc with other interest groups through horse trading of the usual sort so as to influence the shape of legislation. The links between big business and those bourgeois parties that regularly received subsidies from it had enabled its political spokesmen to exert pressure, if not always successfully, on government policies when those parties participated in ruling coalitions. Under the governmental system that began to take shape in 1930, however, the wishes of the business community carried little or no weight with the decisive source of authority, President Hindenburg, or with the military men who served as his counselors. During the period of presidential rule, men chosen by those counselors, men not beholden to big business, determined national policy. And it was those men — Brüning, Papen, and Schleicher — and not Germany's capitalists who set the disastrous political and economic course that destroyed what remained of the Weimar Republic and fostered the growth of the Nazi Party.

If the role of big business in the disintegration of the Republic has been exaggerated, such is even more true of its role in the rise of Hitler. While a significant part of the business community contributed materially — if less than wholly voluntarily — to the consolidation of Hitler's regime after he had become chancellor, he and his party had previously received relatively little support from that quarter. The early growth of the NSDAP took place without any significant aid from the circles of large-scale enterprise. Centered in industrially underdeveloped Bavaria, tainted with illegality as a consequence of the failed beer hall putsch of 1923, saddled with a program containing disturbingly anti-capitalist planks, and amounting only to a raucous splinter group politically, the NSDAP languished in disrepute in the eyes of most men of big business throughout the latter part of the 1920s. The major executives of Germany proved, with rare exception, resistant to the blandishments of Nazis, including Hitler himself, who sought to reassure the business community about their party's intentions. Only the Nazi electoral breakthrough of 1930, achieved without aid from big business, drew attention to it from that quarter. Those businessmen who attempted to assess the suddenly formidable new movement encountered a baffling riddle. The closer they scrutinized the NSDAP, the more difficult it became to determine whether it supported or opposed capitalism and, more specifically, the large-scale, organized enterprise to which capitalism had given rise in Germany. That riddle was not a chance occurrence. Hitler wanted things just that way. By cultivating a strategy of calculated ambiguity on economic matters, he sought to enable the appeals of his party to transcend the deep-seated social divisions in the country. That strategy led to puzzlement and wariness among the politically active components of big business, who wanted above all to establish the NSDAP's position on the economic issues that preoccupied them and assumed ever more urgency as the Great Depression deepened.

For nearly two years — from the autumn of 1930 until the summer of 1932 — elements within or close to big business engaged in flirtations of varying intensity and duration with National Socialism. Some saw in Nazism a potential ally against the political left and organized labor, which many in the business community blamed for much of the country's misfortune, including the depression. Some of those who harbored such hopes set out, often with the help of opportunistic intermediaries, to cultivate prominent figures in the leadership ranks of the NSDAP. On the Nazi side, Hitler and certain of his lieutenants appear to have operated initially on the same assumption that colored leftist analyses, namely, that capitalists amounted to an important factor in politics. But whereas the parties of the left sought to mobilize mass support against big business in order to break the alleged control of the capitalists over the state, Hitler and his accomplices set out merely to neutralize the business community politically in order to keep Germany's capitalists from obstructing the Nazis' grasp for power.

Hitler and other Nazi spokesmen therefore sought repeatedly to convince those capitalists whose ears they could gain that there was no need to fear socialism from National Socialism. In a strict sense that was true, since the Nazis did not seek government ownership of the means of production. But Hitler and other Nazi emissaries revealed only highly selective versions of their movement's aims to members of the business community. They omitted mention of the aspirations of many Nazis, including Hitler himself, for far-reaching changes in German social and economic relationships that would, among other things, have drastically impinged on the position of capitalists. Nor did they, as has often been alleged, promise to dissolve the trade unions, hold out the prospect of lucrative armaments contracts, or project a war of exploitative conquest. The Nazi leaders may have secretly harbored such aims, but to divulge them at a time when the NSDAP was striving to attract voters from all possible quarters and gain admission to the national government would have been out of keeping with their opportunistic tactics. Instead, most portrayed Nazism to the business community as primarily a patriotic movement that would undercut the political left by wooing the wage earners of Germany back into the "national" political camp. Ignoring the concrete economic issues that preoccupied businessmen, Hitler held out to those with whom he came into contact the prospect of a political panacea that would sweep away Germany's mundane problems by unifying it domestically and strengthening it internationally. He also soft-pedaled or left altogether unmentioned his anti-Semitism when speaking to men of big business, having recognized its unpopularity in those circles. Such reassuring versions of the NSDAP's goals generally produced skeptical reactions among members of the business community, however, for those reassurances were offset by clamorous anti-capitalist rhetoric on the part of other Nazis and by the NSDAP's frequent alignment with the political left on concrete socio-economic issues. Right down to Hitler's installation in the chancellorship, Nazism spoke with a forked tongue and behaved duplicitously in the eyes of most capitalist magnates. As a consequence, only rarely did relations between the NSDAP and big business progress beyond the level of flirtation prior to the Nazi takeover. Despite repeated blandishments from Hitler himself and some members of his entourage, most politically active figures in the business community remained confused by the contradictory utterances about economic matters emanating from the NSDAP and uneasy about what direction that party would finally take. Aside from a few minor executives who belonged, for the most part, to the younger generation of Germans so strongly attracted to the Nazi movement, only one capitalist of note, Fritz Thyssen, became a loyal adherent of Nazism before 1933. . . .

Quite contrary to the widespread impression that Hitler gained power in January 1933 with strong backing from big business, his appointment to the chancellorship came just when relations between his movement and the business community had reached the lowest point since the NSDAP's election gains of 1930 had forced it upon the attention of the politically engaged men of big business. Germany's leading capitalists remained passive, ill-informed bystanders during the backroom intrigues in the circles around President Hindenburg that resulted in Hitler's installation as chancellor. By that time the business community was recovering from its initial apprehensions about the cabinet of Kurt von Schleicher. His government had failed to follow the leftward course many had initially feared it would; to the relief of the business community, Schleicher upheld most of the Papen cabinet's policies. While few of the country's capitalists harbored any real enthusiasm for the enigmatic general who stood at the head of the government, an inclination to prefer his continuation in office prevailed in late January 1933. The alternative of still another cabinet crises would, most of the political leadership of big business feared, once more give rise to the uncertainties about economic policy that they believed had thwarted recovery during the politically turbulent year just past. Rather than risk a disruption of the economic upturn widely detected since late 1932, it seemed preferable to hope for a period of stability under the general. When the most prominent industrial association, the Reichsverband, broke with previous practice and attempted to intervene with President Hindenburg as the final cabinet crisis of Weimar Germany broke out at the end of January 1933, it did so to warn against according Adolf Hitler a prominent place in a new, provocatively rightist cabinet. However, that effort to wield the influence of the business community for political purposes proved, like so many undertaken during the Weimar period, in vain.

Contrary to another long-standing misapprehension, spokesmen of the business community did not collude with those of agriculture in agitating for Hitler's installation as chancellor in January 1933. By that time relations between those two interest groups had deteriorated to the breaking point because of increasingly irreconcilable and acrimonious disagreements over trade policy. Whatever took place in early 1933 by way of a recrudescence, in support of Hitler's appointment, of the alliance between traditional elites of the Empire, one important element — big business — was conspicuous by its absence. The often-invoked continuity between the imperial and Nazi regimes thus suffers from a crucial gap.

If big business did not, as is so often maintained, help boost Hitler into the chancellorship by throwing its influence behind him, how much effect did the political money have that flowed from the business community to various Nazis? How much help to Hitler and his party in their quest for power were the contributions and subsidies accounted for here, as well as similar ones that presumably went undocumented? That question can obviously not be answered definitively since the evidence remains incomplete. Some observations can be made, however, on the basis of patterns of behavior that have emerged from this study. First of all, the multi-million-mark contributions from big business that allegedly fueled the Nazi juggernaut existed only in the imaginations of certain contemporary observers and, later, of some writers of history. Those firms and organizations that regularly engaged in large-scale political funding continued — right down to the last election prior to Hitler's appointment as chancellor — to bestow the bulk of their funds on opponents or rivals of the Nazis. The few sizeable contributions that appear to have reached the Nazis from big business sources shrink in significance when compared to the amounts that went to the bourgeois parties and to the campaign to re-elect President Hindenburg. With rare exceptions such contributions to Nazis were not given primarily for the purpose of strengthening the NSDAP or boosting it into power but rather in pursuit of a variety of essentially defensive strategies. They usually went to individual Nazis, not to the party as such. Some of the donors looked upon financial support for prominent Nazis as insurance premiums designed to assure them friends in power if the new movement should succeed in capturing control of the state. Others, who felt that their firms had special grounds to fear the NSDAP if it should come to power, paid out what can only be characterized as protection money to potential rulers. Still others sought to reshape Nazism in line with their wishes by strengthening, through financial subsidies, the position within the party of individual Nazis they regarded as exponents of "moderate" or "reasonable" economic policies. A portion of the subsidies doled out to individual Nazis by men of big business for such reasons may have been used by the recipients for party purposes, but from all indications a considerable share went toward enhancing their personal living standards.

Discussion of financial assistance to the Nazis from big business have usually been based on a false assumption, namely, that the NSDAP, like the bourgeois parties of the Weimar Republic, depended on subsidies from large contributors. This simply was not the case. Just as the Nazi leaders proudly proclaimed at the time, their party financed itself quite handsomely through its own efforts, at least down to the autumn of 1932. The NSDAP proved, in fact, an unprecedentedly effective forerunner of those highly organized fund-raising associations that have since become familiar features of liberal, democratic societies. In contrast to the bourgeois parties of the Republic, whose top echelons solicited large contributions and then distributed funds to the lower echelons, money flowed upward within the NSDAP from the grass roots, through the regional organizations, and to the national leadership in Munich. Compared to the sustained intake of money raised by membership dues and other contributions of the Nazi rank and file, the funds that reached the NSDAP from the side of big business assume at best a marginal significance. As the relations between leading Nazis and members of the business community abundantly reveal, the former rarely adopted the pose of supplicants seeking material aid, at least not until their party experienced its first serious financial difficulties during the autumn of 1932. By that time, however, deteriorating relations had made members of the business community less disposed than ever to contribute to the NSDAP. The Nazis themselves, not Germany's capitalists, provided the decisive financing for Hitler's rise to power. . . .

If the political record of big business is sadly lacking in political acumen, it is even more sorely devoid of public morality and civil courage. Most of the leaders of the business community were never tempted to become Nazis. The NSDAP's promise to destroy the existing elite and impose a new one in its place held little allure for men already at the top of their society. Its plebeian tone offended their taste. So did its anti-Semitism, for whatever other prejudices the leading men of German big business harbored, that form of bigotry was rare in their ranks. Most also found disturbing Nazism's demand for total power and its voluble strain of anti-capitalism, which focused predominantly on large-scale enterprise. Almost as alarming were the unorthodox fiscal and monetary schemes put forward by prominent Nazis as remedies for the depression. Still, most men of big business viewed Nazism myopically and opportunistically. Like many other Germans whose national pride had been wounded by the unexpected loss of the war and by a humiliating peace treaty, they admired Nazism's defiant nationalism and hoped it could be used to help reassert what they regarded as their country's rightful place among the great powers. Preoccupied as they were with domestic economic issues, they also hoped Nazism could be used against their long-standing adversaries, the socialist parties and the trade union movement. That hope waxed and waned as the Nazis shifted their political tactics. During the last half year preceding Hitler's appointment as chancellor, it subsided to low ebb. But few spokesmen of big business spoke out publicly against the NSDAP. Viewing it in terms of narrow self-interest, most failed to perceive the threat it posed to the very foundations of civilized life. Therein lay their heaviest guilt, one they shared, however, with a large part of the German elite.

William Carr

The Cooperation of Big Business

Hitler has often been dismissed as a complete ignoramus in economic matters, a blundering amateur who understood nothing of the intricacies of the subject and cared even less. This is to seriously underestimate him. While it is true that he had no formal training in economics and was certainly not as interested in it as in foreign affairs and military strategy, nevertheless it was an area of public affairs that forced itself on his attention again and again. And because he was alert to the political consequences — or to what he thought were the political consequences of economic decisions — he was able to exert a not inconsiderable influence on broad economic strategy.

Political realism governed Hitler's attitude, and that of other Nazi leaders, to the problem of economic recovery, the most serious challenge facing the new regime. Hitler never doubted for one moment that recovery must be masterminded by the experienced men running German industry and not by party zealots. No sense of gratitude of the

William Carr, *Hitler: A Study in Personality and Politics*, Edward Arnold, London. Reprinted by permission of the publisher.

intervention of agrarian-industrial axis on his behalf dictated this choice. Ever since 1927 he had been seeking contact with big business and fighting "socialist" elements in the party likely to scare off middle-class support. The nearer he came to the chancellery, the more he called unruly elements to order and affirmed his belief in the virtues of (non-Jewish) private enterprise. For a man pathologically suspicious of "bourgeois" professional people, all his life he had a touching regard for the plain bluff entrepreneur whose preeminence in industry he attributed not to inherited wealth and privilege but to the unerring operation of the principle of Social Darwinism.

Hesitation in coming out openly on the side of large-scale industry was due not to lingering doubts about its fitness to effect the recovery or of its rightness to do so, but simply to the exigencies of the confused political situation. Hitler was not master in his own house in the early months of 1933. Many rank-and-file Nazis were agitating for economic change to benefit small retailers and businessmen; party officials bullied employers whenever they could; and middle-class organizations such as NS Hago, the retailer's association, and the Kampfbund für den gewerblichen Mittelstand, or League of Defence for the Commercial Middle Class, were stage-managing noisy campaigns against department stores and consumer cooperatives. Not until the end of May, after the destruction of the trade union movement, did Hitler feel strong enough to come out openly in favour of the traditional masters of German industry. After a meeting with leading industrialists, Hitler readily secured cabinet approval of a most reactionary package deal confirming the blatant class policies of preceding regimes: wages were to be held down to the 1932 levels; industry was promised tax concessions, a reduction in the burden of social payments, and large state contracts; NS Hago and the Kampfbund were called to order; and Wilhelm Keppler, the friend of large-scale industry, replaced Otto Wagener, advocate of the corporate state, as Hitler's party adviser on economic affairs.

In two respects Hitler's personal intervention probably had at least marginal influence on the direction of economic policy in 1933. In the first place, he made it crystal clear from the very beginning that economic recovery must be closely geared to military expansion. This was important for, despite what has been said about the growth of a political "consensus" in favour of a fascist dictatorship, it would be quite wrong to suggest that there was complete identity of viewpoint about the appropriate measures for overcoming the crisis. When Hitler persuaded the cabinet on 8 February to endorse the proposition that the highest priority in any future recovery programme must be given to rearmament for the next five years, he was in effect preparing the way — possibly more quickly than might otherwise have been the case — for a working partnership between heavy industry, army and party, all three of which had an interest in expanding the armed forces as speedily as possible.

Secondly, Hitler's appointment of Schacht as president of the Reichsbank in place of Luther was probably a step of equal importance. Luther was unwilling to provide the massive credits Hitler demanded for the recovery-cum-rearmament programme. Personal preferences apart, Luther's hands were tied because the Reichsbank was effectively controlled by the Bank of International Settlement, set up in 1930 to supervise the payment of reparations under the Young Plan. It was Schacht, a fervent admirer of Hitler and his chief financial adviser since 1931, who solved the problem. Thanks to his international standing, Schacht was able to persuade the bank to allow the Reichsbank to deal in securities again. Of course, although Schacht employed the Keynesian instrument of deficit financing to revive the economy, one need scarcely point out that the object of economic expansion was not the improvement of the living standards of the German people but the thoroughly illiberal one of creating a powerful army to enslave other peoples.

The economic crisis of 1936 and Hitler's intervention in it have been variously interpreted. The reader is reminded that as the demand for raw materials grew to keep pace with the increasing tempo of rearmament, a shortage of foreign exchange developed. In March the insistence of Russia and Roumania on hard cash for their oil precipitated a serious fuel crisis, revealing the precarious nature of the balance of payments. Those sections of industry still interested in export markets together with Schacht's ministry of economics began to express some concern about the direction of the economy. Voices were even raised in favour of retrenchment and some slowdown in the pace of rearmament. Against this background Hitler wrote the celebrated memorandum of August 1936 in which he firmly relegated economic considerations to second place and insisted that, whatever the cost, the highest priority must continue to be given to armaments to ensure that Germany was ready for war by 1940. To obtain the necessary raw materials for this purpose Germany would have to rely less on international trade and rather more on her own autarkical efforts, until such time as she could expand her territory and solve her economic problems at a stroke.

Was this a decisive moment when the dictator's influence changed the course of events? Hardly that. What he was saying in the memorandum simply reflected a significant realignment of forces which took place in the winter of 1935–6. It has been argued that the tacit understanding between party, army command, ministry of economics and heavy industry on which German recovery rested from 1933 onwards, ended in 1936 when the party established its ascendancy over all its rivals forcing them into a policy of accelerated armament, autarky and expansion. This is a somewhat unsatisfactory analysis. A factor of crucial importance overlooked in these interpretations is the decision of army command, taken in the winter of 1935–6 with Hitler's approval, to move on from the construction of a defensive army (not scheduled for completion before 1938) to the creation of an offensive army, which, as originally planned, would not have been ready before 1942. At the same time the existing balance of industrial power was breaking up with the emergence of I. G. Farben as the leading industrial concern in Germany. And I. G. Farben, which had a long-standing interest in the production of synthetic fuel, was strategically placed through close contacts with the air ministry to play a leading role in Goering's attempts to establish autarky. Indeed, the hysterical outbursts in Hitler's memorandum against the cautious orthodoxy of the ministry of economics — where Schacht, though a believer in autarky up to a point, was opposed to a further reduction of Germany's international ties — betrayed some misunderstanding on the Führer's part of the inescapable commitment of much of German industry to continued rearmament. The fact was that by 1936 industry had become so dependent on internal markets that a return to world markets as an alternative to further rearmament was no longer an attractive proposition even if the world economy had been in a healthier state. And more fundamentally the *raison d'être* of the dictatorship would have been destroyed had the Nazis subordinated armaments to the demands of a consumer-goods oriented economy devoted to the raising of the living standards of working people.

It was the coincidence of army plans for rapid expansion with the objective needs of a large part of industry as well as with the vaguely expansionist mood of the party that determined the new course. The first fruits of the refurbished partnership was the Four Year Plan, an exercise in limited autarky. It was announced by Hitler to party comrades at the party rally; it was deeply influenced by the strategic thinking of the Wehrwirtschaftsstab, or military economics staff, of Colonel Thomas; and it was planned by the staff of I. G. Farben. One must conclude, therefore, that Hitler did not take an unexpected initiative in 1936 that changed the course of events, but simply came out on the side of a new alignment of forces which happened to support the option he personally favoured and had pressed for — the creation of an offensive army in the shortest possible time. . . .

It cannot be doubted any more, in the light of recent research, that the economic situation was rapidly deteriorating in 1939. Shortages of raw materials and skilled labour had become critical while government expenditure (chiefly on armaments) continued to grow, thereby creating dangerous inflationary pressures. Publicly, Hitler obstinately refused to accept the facts of economic life. To keep on insisting on the highest priority for armaments seemed to show no appreciation of the harsh choice that would have to be made sooner or later to avert economic collapse. On the other hand, it may well be that his sensitive antennae detected with uncanny accuracy the unavoidable political consequences of a steadily deteriorating situation. As he told the Reichstag in January 1939: "In the final instance the economy of the Reich today is bound up with its external security. It is better to see that while there is still time as when it is too late." In his address to the commanding generals on 22 August, he was brutally frank about the interdependence of economic policy and foreign policy: "We have nothing to lose, only to gain. As a result of restrictions our economic situation is such that we can only hold out for a few years. Goering can confirm that. There is nothing else for it, we have to act." In other words, Hitler probably realized that the maintenance of the mobilization capacity of German industry at its present high level for an indefinite period was virtually impossible once the peacetime needs of the armed forces were met. If large-scale arms exports were impossible and if the economic and social disruption consequent upon a switch to the production of other goods was unacceptable, then Germany was left with a clear choice — either to continue to endure mounting inflation to defray the astronomical costs of further rearmament or to create a fresh demand for armaments by waging war.

Having said this, one must also admit quite frankly that there is far too little positive evidence to permit us to determine with any degree of accuracy the importance of such considerations in Hitler's decision for war. Serious though the internal situation was in 1939, one cannot say with absolute certainty that it was impossible for Germany to wait any longer before going to war. One cannot discount the possibility that the steadily deteriorating situation — of which Hitler was kept informed — may have done little more than confirm his own pessimistic long-term diagnosis of Germany's ills and strengthen the case for a war of conquest which he deemed necessary in any case on politico-ideological grounds. It may well be that within a year or two economic pressures would have forced Hitler's hand. What we do not have is sufficient evidence that this was the case in 1939.

It is even more difficult to determine the role of the great industrial combines in setting Germany on the road to war and in nudging Hitler towards expansion. It seems fairly clear that because industry retained, broadly speaking, the essentials of economic independence at a time or rapid industrial concentration, firms such as the Mannesmann-Konzern, the Reichswerke Hermann Goering and I. G. Farben, all closely associated with rearmament, and leading banks, especially the Dresden and Deutsche Banken, were in a position to develop their own expansionist plans for the domination of central and southeastern European markets. Of course these plans did not necessitate the forcible absorption of surrounding territories in the Reich for their realization. Industrial imperialism and territorial imperialism were distinctive plants. Nevertheless, they were nurtured in the same soil and each was closely affected by the other's growth. Domination of central and southeastern Europe was also a Nazi objective both to attain economic self-sufficiency (the *Grossraumwirtschaft*) and to serve as a base for a future *Drang nach Osten* or Thrust to the East. On this practical foundation a working partnership came into being. There is evidence of this partnership in action both in Austria and Czechoslovakia where certain industrial corporations were able to secure a dominant position in the economics of these countries in 1938–9. To establish more precisely what the relationship was between the forward thrust of the great industrial combines controlling the German economy and the expansionist policies of the Nazi hierarchy in 1938–9 we need much more information than we have at present about the policies of individual firms. Provisionally, all that one can say is that economic imperialism on its own would not necessarily have led to war — and did not do so in other capitalist economies. It was only in conjunction with the territorial imperialism of the Nazis that economic imperialism developed "a particularly explosive power."

Ernst Christian Helmreich

The Ambiguity of Religious Leaders

Neither the Protestant nor the Catholic church broke with their heritage from the past during the Weimar Republic. But this is not to say that they remained static. Changes were made which largely continued trends that had already been developing under the Empire. Although the Weimar Constitution boldly proclaimed, "There is no state church," this did not mean that the close relations between the state and church were broken. While the churches became more self-governing, their self-rule was administered under the supervision of the state. The Land churches and the Catholic church, as well as a growing number of the Free churches, were public corporations, and by their very status were subject to some state regulations.

The Protestant churches had, during the Weimar period, given themselves new governing bodies, and laws, orders, and regulations had multiplied, as had the bureaucracy which administered them. It is easy to decry this extensive legalism and emphasize its stultifying effect on church life, but it did mean that the churches on the whole were well run, and that their rights and privileges were founded in law. This legal foundation was very valuable when the Nazis tried arbitrarily to bend the churches to their will. The courts, particularly in the early years of Hitler's rule, decided many appealed cases in favor of churchmen on the basis of law and established procedures. And it was not only the courts which at times stayed Nazi hands. The often maligned bureaucrats, the civil servants who staffed the various state departments and bureaus in charge of religious and cultural affairs, often continued to run things in customary ways to the benefit of the churches. Accustomed to carrying on an orderly procedure, they opposed the irregular innovations of newly installed Nazi officials. The penchant for order and law did not disappear at once in Germany, not even among the Nazis.

From *The German Churches under Hitler: Background, Struggle, and Epilogue*, by Ernst Christian Helmreich. Copyright © 1979 by Wayne State University Press. Reprinted by permission of the publisher and the author.

But there is more to a church than its organization and the admin-istration of its institutional affairs, important as these matters are in large church bodies. Churches are made up of people; they are a part of society and are beset by all the problems which confront a nation. The Catholic church, through its close ties with the Center party and the Bavarian People's party, had been forced more than ever to share and bear political responsibilities. A government party throughout most of the days of the republic, the Center party nevertheless had many sup-porters, especially in the church hierarchy, who looked back to monarchical days with a certain longing. In Protestant church circles many were conservatively inclined and ready to discard existing parlia-mentary political forms and practices. To point this out is to say nothing more than that the churches were composed of Germans not yet firmly attached to their new form of government. The hardships, the sins of the times, were all too easily blamed on the government which, many Germans felt, needed to be changed and set on new paths.

But if the government needed reform, and there were few Germans no matter what their political allegiance who doubted it, so too did the churches. Within the Catholic church, hierarchically led and true to Rome, the demand for regeneration was not pronounced among the laity, nor could it easily make itself felt. The hierarchy, by no means complacent, were aware that there was much to be done to strengthen the church, and they were all too willing to seek government support in this task. Catholics as a whole were eager to manifest their loyalty to Germany. When the Nazis found increasing acceptance of their claim to be the true repository of patriotism, many rank-and-file Catholics felt their loyalty to state and nation was being jeopardized by the church's continued support of the Catholic parties and their denunciations of national socialism. The patriotic desire not to stand aside while Ger-many was being rebuilt was probably the factor most influential in bringing about the initial peaceful relations between both Catholic and Protestant churches and national socialism when Hitler became chan-cellor.

The papacy and members of the German hierarchy in the pre-war years had at times denounced the cult of racism, of blood and soil. But there were no clarion protests against the anti-Semitic policy of the Nazi rulers then or during the war years. When the government began to treat Christians who were racial Jews in the same way as full Jews, the Catholic church leaders — concerned about safeguarding their own, began to take more notice. In general their reaction was similar to that of the Protestant leaders, but there were some noteworthy Catholic reactions. For example, the decree of September 1, 1941, which required all Jews to wear a Star of David, prompted Cardinal Bertram to send advice to his fellow bishops. Guenther Lewy has summarized it admirably.

> His council was to avoid "rash measures that could hurt the feelings of the Jewish Catholics, as the introduction of special Jewish benches, separation when administering the sacraments, introduction of special services in specific churches or private houses." The segregation of the Catholic non-Aryans would violate Christian principles, and, therefore, should be avoided as long as possible. The priests, Bertram suggested, might however advise the Jewish Catholics to attend the early mass whenever possible. An admonishment to the faithful to exercise brotherly love toward the non-Aryans similarly should be postponed until disturbances resulted. "Only when substantial difficulties result from attendance at church by the non-Aryan Catholics," the Archbishop of Breslau continued, "(like staying away of officials, Party members and others, demonstrative leaving of divine services), should the Catholic non-Aryans be consulted about the holding of special services." In case a reminder to the faithful to treat the Jewish Catholics with love should become necessary, Bertram suggested a statement that included St. Paul's admonishments to the Romans and Galatians not to forget that among those believing in Christ there is neither Jew nor Greek, for all are one in Jesus Christ (Romans 10:12, Galatians 3:28).

Bertram was certainly not recommending a courageous policy but one of servile accommodation: the presence of officials and party members was more desirable than that of a hard-pressed Christian of non-Aryan descent seeking solace and redemption in God's word. In much the same vein, Bishops Berning and Wienken tried to obtain permission for Jewish Catholics not to wear the star when they went to church; apparently they were not very concerned about other times. The Gestapo, as on other occasions, operated with an even hand — even if it was a damnable one — and refused to make any alterations in their general edict. Actually the people in the churches caused no difficulties, although Jewish Christians often did refrain from attending church.

In the end the problem of racial segregation never became acute in the churches, partly because so many Christian Jews were deported. On the other hand, both Catholic and Protestant churches (no doubt unwilling but without strong protest) did succumb to the government's extreme racial segregation measures against the Poles.

In 1942 the government began considering a plan to force the dissolution of racially mixed marriages. This compulsory divorce policy would affect a large number of Catholics and challenged one of the most important doctrines of the church. Cardinal Bertram addressed letters of protest to the ministers of justice, the interior, and ecclesiastical affairs. Bishop Wurm and other Protestant leaders also protested. The compulsory divorce law was never issued, perhaps because of ecclesiastical protest, but perhaps also because some hundreds of Aryan wives demonstrated in Berlin when their non-Aryan husbands were about to be transported "to the East."

The most compelling factor in easing policies towards the churches was the disastrous course of the war. On February 2, 1943, Stalingrad surrendered, the beginning of May brought German defeat in North Africa, July 10 the invasion of Sicily, July 25 the fall of Mussolini, September 3 the invasion of southern Italy, and five days later the announcement of the Italian armistice. On September 10 German troops took over the occupation of Rome. Such sledgehammer blows clearly called for a united home front, and measures were taken to decrease internal tensions.

On January 13, 1943, Hitler had issued an ordinance, "The Employment of Men and Women in Tasks of National Defense." It specifically exempted clergymen and monastic priests, others who were in the service of churches forty-eight hours a week, and nurses or members of monastic orders fully employed in agriculture. On April 26, 1943, Bormann issued a special directive on dealing with political-confessional matters. Nothing was to be done to cause confessional difficulties or unrest among the people. "Every little pinprick policy must be stopped." On May 9, Bormann expressly forbade any agitation against the churches in the Labor Service: "One must carefully avoid injuring true religious conceptions. Such actions simply antagonize the best persons. . . . It is entirely wrong — and therefore fundamentally forbidden in the National Labor Service — to enter upon any polemic against church institutions and dogmas." The Labor Service was not a church but a state service, whose duty it was to unify, not divide, the people.

In February, 1939, Heydrich as head of the security service had prepared a long memorandum on Catholic higher schools for the training of priests in which he proposed cuts in state support. The memorandum was considered again on July 19, 1943, when it was decided that nothing should be done about it.

At this time German cities were being subjected to heavy bombing; Hamburg was virtually destroyed at the end of July, with a death toll estimated at around 40,000. This bombing led the minister of education, with Bormann's approval, to issue a directive on August 25, 1943, concerning confessional religious instruction at schools which had been evacuated. It was most favorable to the traditional demands of the churches. Confessional instruction was to be given to the same extent as before, and teachers were to be moved with the school if possible. If no religion teachers were available, local clergymen were to be asked to give confessional instruction in local church rooms and to issue certificates to pupils. If local regulations permitted, religious instruction could be given in other rooms as well, if they were not more than four kilometers from the place to which the school had been moved. His intention to conciliate the churches is clearly shown in his closing plea: "Please take care that in administering this directive you observe a generous line of action."

Going easy on the churches was on the whole the policy during the rest of the war. As the ring was drawn more tightly around Germany and collapse threatened, the churches also tended to make a few difficulties as possible for the state. It is clear that the hierarchy were aware of the deportation of Jews and what it meant. Yet the German bishops never spoke out as Dutch, Belgian, or French bishops did when Jews were being transported from their countries. The nearest the hierarchy came to a joint protest was the Fulda pastoral letter of September 12, 1943, "Ten Commandments as Laws of Life for Nations." In the introduction the bishops recognized the critical situation the Reich was facing and spoke words of tribute and encouragement to the Catholic faithful. By way of commentary on the individual commandments they could make many pointed statements without directly attacking the government. Cardinal Bertram objected, but it was nevertheless read in Catholic pulpits. It was the last joint pastoral letter issued by the German bishops during the Hitler era. The police summary on the letter lacked the customary sharp denunciations and concluded: "in no other pastoral letter was the span of its possible effects between positive and negative so great as in this case." The bishops clearly had done a remarkable job of tightrope walking.

The statement on the Fifth Commandment, "Thou shall not kill," while it was directed against the gas ovens and the killing of Jews, nevertheless was not worded openly and fearlessly. There was no indication of the magnitude of the Nazi extermination policy, although the hierarchy must have had some knowledge of what was going on. The bishops, as well as the government, were concerned about maintaining "internal unity" during the war. After commenting that no one had the right arbitrarily to interfere with God's power over life and death, the bishops declared:

> *Killing is bad in itself, even when it is done in the interest of the common welfare: against innocent and defenseless mentally ill and other sick; against incurable invalids and fatally injured, against those with inherited disabilities and children with serious birth defects, against innocent hostages and disarmed war and other prisoners; against people of alien race and descent. Even the government can and is permitted to punish with the death penalty only those who are truly death-deserving criminals.*

Here the bishops made no distinction between Christian Jews and other Jews. However, the former were always their chief concern, as they were when the Vatican came to protesting the deportation of Hungarian Jews in 1944. There were a few who took a broader view. Foremost among them was Provost Bernhard Lichtenberg in Berlin, who spoke up against anti-Semitism and daily said a prayer for all Jews, not only the baptized ones. He was arrested in 1941 and died while being transported to Dachau in 1943. Others sought to protect and help various individual Jews. No one, however, has successfully contradicted Lewy's conclusion: "In sharp contrast to the countries of western Europe, in Germany only a handful of Jews were hidden by the [Catholic] clergy or otherwise helped by them in their hour of distress." The churchmen, as probably most of their congregations (and as 99 percent of all postwar Germans aver), did not approve of the government's rabid policy, but they were inclined to play it safe and not do much about it. The cannonball of anti-Semitism had started rolling down the hill many years in the past, no one bothered to stay its momentum after 1933, and when the war came it dragged Germany with increasing acceleration into a moral abyss.

Catholicism always involves not only the laity and the hierarchy, with its leadership of the local churches, but also the papacy. And papal policy was not very different from that of the German people or the German hierarchy. The pope too played it safe. His very international position forced him into a policy of neutrality and impartiality at the start of the war. He had sought to prevent the hostilities, and then his attention was bent on restoring peace. His was not an enviable position, and the involvement of the Soviet Union and later the United States made it no easier. Whatever he said and did in public would be held against him by one side or another. He naturally fell back on diplomatic procedures, on confidential negotiations with the responsible governments, in which he had long years of practice. He instructed his nuncio to raise constant protests in Germany about wartime policies; he sought to alleviate the suffering caused by the war. In his efforts to achieve peace he even went so far as to offer his good offices (1939–40) to German resistance leaders in their approach to British authorities. He did seek to prevent the deportation of Jews in Italy, Hungary, and other countries. In the realm of diplomacy, in his efforts to achieve things from behind the public scene, the pope did not remain silent or inactive. On the other hand, he was indeed circumspect in his public utterances in his efforts to maintain official impartiality. The history of World War I also showed that it was easy to be misled as to what was propaganda and what was reality. Unfortunately, the war atrocities were true this time, and the pope never issued a solemn public indictment. There were many other things he might have denounced, such as saturation bombing by both sides and the killing of thousands of defenseless men, women, and children. Perhaps such a protest might have been effective, but perhaps Hitler, and other wartime leaders as well, would have raised the same question Stalin was reputed to have asked: "How many divisions does he [the Pope] have?"

That a ringing denunciation of Hitler's policies would have made the situation of the Catholics in general, and of the Catholic church in particular, more difficult in Germany is doubtful, considering the plans Hitler had in mind for the future of the churches anyway. Yet the possibility of evoking immediate harsh retaliatory measures was always taken into consideration at the Vatican. That a public papal plea for the Jews would have led to an effective upsurge of Catholic opposition to the National Socialist regime seems most unlikely. That it would have led to a worldwide crusade against Hitler's tyranny is improbable and in fact inconsequential, for the mass of the available manpower of the world was already enrolled under the banner of the United Nations. What would have happened had the pope spoken out more openly than he did, is speculative; speculation may be interesting, but it is hardly historical. However, some things are historically clear. The pope and the German hierarchy worked closely together in the war years as they had in former periods of German history; the hierarchy did not beseech the pope to speak out during the war as they did in August, 1936, and at the time of the encyclical *Mit brennender Sorge* (1937). Neither hierarchy nor pope ran away, none succumbed, none won crowns of martyrdom; all lived on to fight for their faith another day.

Hans-Adolf Jacobsen

Military Officers and the Resistance

At the end of 1942, the disaster at Stalingrad, followed by that some days later at El Alamein, justified the forecasts of the politico-military conspirators. Beck succeeded in contacting Paulus and begged him to address a message to Germany and the world denouncing the criminal folly of the Berchtesgaden madman. Paulus appeared to hesitate. At any rate he was silent.

On April 5, 1943, three of Oster's best collaborators in Counterintelligence were arrested — Joseph Müller, Hans von Dohnanyi and the pastor Dietrich Bonhoeffer. Oster was dismissed. The Security Service (the "SD") obtained the dissolution of the Abwehr, its sworn enemy. This bastion of the Resistance was, therefore, destroyed. The deaths in 1943 of General von Hammerstein-Equord and the Socialist leader Carlo Mierendorff also constituted two great losses for the Cause.

Thanks, however, to a few men at the Eastern front, replacements were forthcoming — General Henning von Tresckow, Chief of Staff of an Army Group, and his friends Gersdorff and von Schlabrendorff. On March 13, 1943, Tresckow placed a bomb in Hitler's aircraft as the Führer was making one of his rare visits to the Russian front. The mechanism failed. Two other attempts to destroy the Führer came to grief because at the last minute he had cancelled his planned visit.

At the end of 1943, the young Colonel Claus Schenk von Stauffenberg, who had been seriously wounded in the war, accepted with enthusiasm Olbricht's proposition to strike at the tyrant. He was prepared to sacrifice his life for the Cause. Stauffenberg, a noble Swabian, a

From *The German Opposition to Hitler as Viewed by Foreign Historians: An Anthology*, edited by Hans-Adolf Jacobsen.

fervent Catholic and mystic, was imbued not with the militarism of the Germany of the Kaisers but with the Christian traditions of the Holy Roman Empire of old.

The conspirators prepared a plan known as "Valkyrie" to be launched immediately after the attempted assassination had taken place. It envisaged alerting the forces of the interior, the arrest of the Party chiefs, the disarming of the S.S. formations, the occupation of vital points — notably the radio stations — and the liberation of the concentration camp inmates.

A provisional Government was to be established, with Beck Head of State, Goerdeler Chancellor, and Witzleben Commander-in-Chief of the Armed Forces. A proclamation to the German people and the Armed Forces was prepared and the draft of a liberal Constitution elaborated. Negotiations for peace were immediately to be solicited of the Anglo-Saxons.

Though the conspirators were limited in number, they were truly national because they included military, Conservative and Socialist elements — Beck and Witzleben, Goerdeler and von Hassell, Leuschner and Leber.

The Commandant of Paris, General von Stülpnagel, had been firmly won over to the conspiracy. His adjutant, Colonel Cäsar von Hofacker, a cousin of Stauffenberg, constituted the liaison between Paris and Berlin. Rommel, Commander of Army Group B, had also been persuaded to join the opposition.

Leber and his friend Reichwein increased their efforts so that the Socialist and trade union cells would prevail on the masses to support the military coup. Alas! Betrayed by a police informer, the two men were arrested at the beginning of June, and Rommel, wounded on July 17, disappeared for ever from the scene.

For the plotters, it was now a matter of launching the attack at the first possible moment. One favourable circumstance seemed to bring it nearer. At the beginning of July, Stauffenberg was appointed Chief of Staff to General Fromm, who was in command of the forces of the interior. Fromm was quite sympathetic to the movement — always provided it succeeded! As part of his new duties, Stauffenberg had periodically to make a report to the Führer at his headquarters in East Prussia, and this would allow him to strike there.

The events of that fateful July 20 are well-known. Stauffenberg appeared at the conference, placed his brief case containing the time bomb under the table, left the room, saw an explosion and believed in good faith that it had succeeded. Three of those present were killed, about fifteen wounded — some mortally like Schmundt, one of the Führer's intimates. Hitler himself received only bruises. Stauffenberg returned by air to Berlin and told Beck of his success. The Valkyrie Plan was set in motion, but Fromm asked for confirmation by telephone of Stauffenberg's statements, to be told by Keitel in person that the Führer was safe and sound.

The events then followed one another with the precision of an axe and the inevitability of a film. The miserable Fromm summoned the S.S. Beck committed suicide. Olbricht, Stauffenberg and his friends Merz von Quirnheim and Werner von Haeften were executed on the spot after the mockery of a trial. Before the salvo was fired Stauffenberg cried "Long live our sacred Germany!"

On July 21 von Tresckow committed suicide. He was followed on July 26 by Colonel Baron Wessel von Freytagh-Loringhoven, who had supplied the bomb for Stauffenberg. And then came the wholesale arrest of all the plotters.

When, at 4 p.m. on July 20 in Paris, Stülpnagel received Stauffenberg's message announcing Hitler's death, he gave the orders that had been prepared months beforehand and had all the members of the Security Service and the S.S. arrested, together with their chief, General Oberg. Under the eyes of the astonished Parisians, the soldiers threw themselves on the Party men. Thus, for a brief moment, the German Resistance was transferred to Paris! Stülpnagel and Hofacker prepared to report to Montgomery. They hoped that Kluge, the Commander-in-Chief in the West, who gave them encouragement, would be won over to the Cause under the influence of Speidel, his Chief of Staff, who had already joined the Resistance.

Alas! When the actual result of the attempted assassination became known, not only did Kluge not move, despite the efforts of Stülpnagel, who decided to act all the same, but he sent Hitler a telegram protesting his loyalty. From then, all was lost. And Stülpnagel's dreadful end is known. He shot himself through the head, became blind, was operated upon and then cared for, all the better to bring him to trial and martyr him afterwards. Four weeks later he was hanged. Hofacker was subjected to atrocious torture before being executed on December 20.

The coup d'état, an act of desperation, had only a minute chance of succeeding — ten per cent., thought one of the resisters, Cäsar von Hofacker, who was, however, entirely dedicated.

In the event, the big military chiefs "did not march". On the

Eastern front, none of the three Army Group commanders joined in, despite the entreaties of Tresckow and others. In the West, Rundstedt was opposed to all action, and his successor, Kluge, was merely a coward. Rommel, as we know, was no longer there. In France one could only count on Stülpnagel, his adjutant Cäsar von Hofacker, and Eberhard Finckh, apart from a few subalterns. At home, Fromm, the Commander-in-Chief, was merely an opportunist. Only about a dozen generals in command of active units, such as Olbricht and Hase, showed any determination. All were executed. Beck, Witzleben, Hoepner and Oster were no longer in the Army.

In the Armed Forces, as among the population generally, there were some brave local groups, though there was no extensive or coordinated organization at all. Since, following the reverses, the air raids and privation, discontent prevailed, the majority of the people would, without any doubt, have hailed the death of Hitler. But how to bring about a general uprising? The Party units were powerful, fierce, and persecuted without mercy. Amid the frightful ruins to which the towns had been reduced, every one was wholly dependent on the régime for food cards and all objects essential to life. . . .

The accused were spared nothing . . . torture, lashes with the whip, privation of sleep, reprisals on their families, the most degrading insults. There was no appeal against the verdict, and hanging was done on the spot. No priest was present to give solace to the men in their agony. The trials and executions were filmed, with Hitler ordering the films to be presented to him so that he could indulge in a welter of sadism. The President of the Court, Rudolf Freisler, outdid Fouquier-Tinville in horror. He subjected the accused to vile insults. The spectacle he provoked was so abject that the Minister of Justice, Thierack, although a convinced Nazi, wrote to Hitler's secretary, Martin Bormann, saying that the President's behaviour "produces a profoundly disagreeable impression. The gravity and dignity of the Court have suffered under it. Freisler is entirely lacking in the frigid and calm reserve that alone are appropriate for such a trial." . . .

It seems likely that there were 5,000 people, 2,000 of them army officers, who died as a result of persecution following July 20. A great many of the condemned were executed shortly after the pronouncement of the verdict. The others, even more unfortunate, had for many months to submit to the severest cruelties and were then massacred by the S.S. at Flossenburg in April, 1945, only a few hours before the arrival of the American troops.

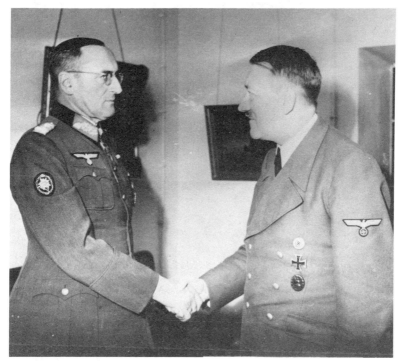

Hitler at the End. Hitler, his left arm still lame from the unsuccessful attempt on his life, congratulates Colonel General (four-star general) Schoerner, whom he had just appointed commander-in-chief of a crumbling and practically nonexistent Wehrmacht. (Wide World Photos)

As for Freisler, the President of the "People's Court", he was mortally injured, "as if by a judgment of God", on one of the last days of the trials in full view of the Court when a beam fell from the ceiling following an air raid on Berlin by the Royal Air Force.

After July 20 the Resistance was very much weakened. The fight was carried on by a few groups of determined people, such as that of Lieutenant Rupprecht Gerngross which was known under the name of "Freedom Action Bavaria". On April 28, 1945, the Gerngross men attacked the local Nazis of Munich, seized the vital points in the city, hoisted the white flag, and allowed the Bavarian capital to be occupied by the Allies without a shot being fired and without loss.

The Survivors. These starving men, survivors of the German concentration camp at Nordhausen, were among the tiny minority of those who entered the camps and lived to tell the tale of mass extermination. Their eyes tell of the horror they have seen. (UPI/Bettmann Newsphotos)

138

The Social Impact of Nazism

Variety of Opinion

The major initiative clearly came from local leaders. It would be extremely interesting to know exactly what means were used by the NSDAP to instill the sense of purposefulness and initiative into its local groups.

William Sheridan Allen

The full weight of the intricate machinery of state was brought directly and suddenly to bear upon the working population.

T. W. Mason

These alternative forms of social behaviour within the Third Reich show that considerable sections of the younger generation held themselves aloof from National Socialism.

Detlev Peukert

Women's group activity developed something of a split personality because it embraced these different kinds of women. It also started and grew spontaneously and in a varitey of forms because the inherent male chauvinism of the movement led to exclusive concentration on the men's struggle.

Jill Stephenson

> Revolutionaries have never been popular in Germany, and Hitler
> would never have had the full aura of legitimacy he needed had he taken
> power by force. Accordingly, Nazi violence and illegality after Hitler
> became chancellor were widely condemned.
>
> Sarah Gordon

*Our final problem concerns the coordination (Gleichschaltung) of Ger-
man society by the Nazi regime. This term connotes an effort by the state
to penetrate all aspects of public life and to leave private as little as
possible. Every organization and every individual were to march to the
same beat. Those who were reluctant would be goaded. Those who refused would be eliminated.*

*William Sheridan Allen takes us to a small town of twenty
thousand in the vicinity of Hannover. Because Northeim was a rail
junction and an administrative center with a large number of state
employees, it was admittedly not typical in its extreme vulnerability to
Nazism. Yet it nonetheless illustrated how important the sheer vitality of
its local organizations was to Nazism. When economic crisis induced a
polarization of society, the town's broad middle class tended to the right
rather than to the left, embracing the Nazi party while rejecting the
"radical" Social Democrats. Allen first explains the irrational nature of
this fateful option and then analyzes its consequences. Old allegiances
and activities soon disappeared and the Swastika alone prevailed.*

*T. W. Mason picks up the story of the German labor movement
following the abolition of trade unions in May 1933, just four months
after Hitler's seizure of power. The trade unions were replaced by the
unified German Labor Front, led by Robert Ley. This innovation indicated the need of Nazism for the cooperation of German workers if
industry were to fulfill the task of preparing the nation for a possible war.
The Labor Front thus undertook a massive job of persuasion, encourag-
ing workers to find "Strength through Joy." This slogan meant, among
other things, more organized holidays, sports, folk dancing, and theater
presentations — all under the watchful eye of the party. But with the
advent of the war, many workers were mobilized, production quotas were
increased, and the strain in the workplace began to tell. The inevitable
result, Mason shows, was a militarization of the labor force. The full
meaning of dictatorship became painfully evident, and the joy was soon
gone.*

Detlev Peukert *chronicles the fate of young people in the Third Reich. Initially the Hitler Youth and its female counterpart* (Bund deutscher Mädel) *seemed to be just a peculiarly German form of scouting, with an emphasis on camping, sports, and harmless fun. But in time these organizations became bureaucratized and militarized, which was not to every adolescent's liking. Dissatisfaction with officially sponsored groups produced a youthful protest movement not unlike the gangs of American inner cities. Peukert identifies two of them: the "Edelweiss Pirates" and the "Swing Youth." Although different in style, they shared a disdain for the frantic patriotism and puritan morality of their do-gooding peers. Even in a Nazi state, it seems, the sex drive of the young was irrepressible and dictatorship had its limits.*

Jill Stephenson *concentrates on the role of German women, thousands of whom had begun to enter the labor force well before the First World War. By abandoning or altering their traditional social functions as homemakers and mothers, they provoked the criticism that they were damaging the quality of the race. This, at any rate, was the Nazi view, which Stephenson characterizes as blatant male chauvinism. Not all women were enchanted with a place on the pedestal or in the nursery. Female dissenters responded in a variety of ways. Some women stubbornly resisted Nazi blandishments; many remained loyal to their church; and others were simply indifferent. Hence, Stephenson concludes, the attempt to "coordinate" women under one state directorate had only limited success.*

Sarah Gordon *stresses the high degree of integration attained by German Jews before 1933. Even Hitler found that anti-Semitism was not unduly popular in the 1920s, and he was forced to tone down that aspect of his political propaganda. Blaming Jews for all the ills of the nation nevertheless remained crucial to the theory and practice of Nazism; once in power, Hitler proved it. A process of dis-integration of the Jews began: first exclusion, then expulsion, and finally extermination. Gordon doubts that the majority of the German people supported such measures. She considers that the infamous "Night of the Broken Glass"* (Kristallnacht) — *the first concerted physical violence against the Jews in 1938 — was actually a failure on the part of the Nazis. Yet no vigorous and widespread protest against the violence was evident. Once started, therefore, the killing could continue until Nazi Germany created Auschwitz.*

Once again we find that the historical record is full of contradic-

tions. The social reality of the Nazi revolution did not fit any simple theory. To understand such a phenomenon, we must remain alert to its complexity. Surely easy generalizations and uninformed prejudices should have no place in our study of Nazism.

William Sheridan Allen

The Nazification of a Town

Northeim is not now, and never was, a "typical" German town. The composition of Northeim in Weimar and Nazi days was not the same as the rest of Germany. There were an inordinate number of civil servants and the town was dominated economically by the railroad. Few places in Germany began the Third Reich with a two-thirds vote for the NSDAP, the national average being on the order of two-fifths. On the other hand, there were many places in Germany that saw more violence than Northeim in the early days of the Third Reich.

What, then, is to be learned from Northeim's experience in the Nazi years?

In the first place, it is clear that an essential arena in the Nazi electoral surge and the seizure of power was on the local level, and that the critical figures were the local Nazi leaders. Northeim's Nazis created their own image by their own initiative, vigor, and propaganda. They knew exactly what needed to be done to effect the transfer of power to themselves in the spring of 1933, and they did it without more than generalized directives from above. Exactly how much was initiated locally and how much was promoted by the example of other Nazi groups in other towns or by the District and national Nazi leadership cannot yet be fully determined. Certainly there were no written orders from above, though there may have been verbal ones. But the major initiative clearly came from local leaders. It would be extremely inter-

From *The Nazi Seizure of Power: The Experience of a Single German Town, 1922–1945*, rev. ed., William Sheridan Allen. Copyright © 1965, 1984 by William Sheridan Allen. Reprinted with permission of Franklin Watts, Inc.

esting to know exactly what means were used by the NSDAP to instill the sense of purposefulness and initiative into its local groups, which were then used by the movement as a whole. It would be useful to know in explicit detail how coordination was combined with flexibility in this authoritarian instrument. The material available for this study of Northeim did not supply complete answers to these questions. It has, however, made clear that there would have been no Nazi revolution in Northeim, at least not of the totality that has been described here, without an active and effective local organization. Hitler, Goebbels, and the other Nazi leaders provided the political decisions, ideology, national propaganda, and, later, the control over the government that made the revolution possible. Hitler also gave his followers a simple goal that no other party shared: the idea of taking total and exclusive power at the first chance. But it was in the hundreds of localities like Northeim all over Germany that the revolution was made actual. They formed the foundation of the Third Reich.

As for the reasons behind the particular experience in Northeim, the most important factor in the victory of Nazism was the active division of the town along class lines. Though there was cohesion in Northeim before the Nazis began their campaigns leading to the seizure of power, the cohesion existed within the middle class or within the working class and did not extend to the town as a whole. The victory of Nazism can be explained to a large extent by the desire on the part of Northeim's middle class to suppress the lower class and especially its political representatives, the Social Democratic party. Nazism was the first effective instrument for this.

This is why Northeimers rejoiced in the gains of the Nazis and this is why they applauded the institution of the dictatorship. The antipathy of the middle class was not directed toward individual members of the SPD, but only toward the organization itself; not toward the working class as such, but only toward its political and social aspirations; not, finally, toward the reality of the SPD, but mainly toward a myth that they nurtured about the SPD. For a variety of reasons, Northeim's middle class was so intent on dealing a blow to the Social Democrats that it could not see that the instrument it chose would one day be turned against itself.

Exactly why Northeimers were so bitterly opposed to the Socialists cannot be answered on the basis of a study of this town alone; the answer lies in the history and social structure of Imperial and Weimar

Germany, and possibly can be given only by a social psychologist. Nevertheless it seems clear that the nature of the SPD had something to do with the burghers' attitudes. Northeim's Socialists maintained slogans and methods which had little correspondence with reality. They maintained the façade of a revolutionary party when they were no longer prepared to lead a revolution. They never seriously attempted to mend fences with the middle class and frequently offended bourgeois sensibilities by their shortsightedness and shallow aggressiveness.

Yet it would be wholly incorrect to place all the blame upon Northeim's Social Democracy. The middle class responded to the existence of the SPD in ways which were almost paranoid. Its members insisted upon viewing the SPD as a "Marxist" party at a time when this was no longer so. They were determined to turn the clock back to a period when the organized working class was forcibly kept from exerting influence. They felt threatened by the very existence of this organization. This view of the SPD was not in accord with reality, since by any objective standard the goal of the SPD in Northeim was to maintain the kind of town that Northeim's middle class itself wanted.

What was needed in Northeim to stop the Nazis was a political coalition of the decent people, regardless of party, to recognize that — whatever it promised — Nazism was an indecent thing. That such a coalition never developed was the main reason the Nazis got into power. But it was the middle class that gave them their chance.

Perhaps the behavior of the good burghers of Northeim becomes more understandable when one realizes the extent to which they were committed to nationalism. The excess of patriotic feeling in the town during the pre-Hitler period was the great moral wedge for Nazism. In many ways the actions and beliefs of Northeimers during the last years of the Weimar era were the same as if World War I had never ended. It was in this sort of atmosphere that the SPD might seem treasonable and the Nazi reasonable.

A similar effect was wrought by the depression. While Northeim's middle class was not decisively affected by the economic crisis, the burghers were made desperate through fear and through an obsession with the effects of the depression, especially the sight of the unemployed. As for the effect of the depression upon the lower classes, it was equally large. There is no doubt that the progressive despair of the jobless, as reflected in the longer and longer periods of unemployment, weakened the forces of democracy in the town. It may be that this

Heim ins Reich. Hitler realizes one of his fondest ambitions by claiming his native Austria as part of the new Germany. Here he arrives at the city limits of Vienna in March 1938 and receives only the beginning of a triumphant welcome. (Wide World Photos)

sapped the SPD's will to fight and led it into ritualistic responses to Nazism. It was hard for Socialists to bend all their efforts to combating Nazism when this involved defending a system that could produce this sort of economic misery. Had the SPD seriously undertaken to introduce democratic socialism in response to the depression, it seems likely they would have found new sources of strength among their own followers, and very likely might have won the votes of the many Northeimers who cast ballots for the NSDAP simply because the Nazis promised to end the depression. In short, intelligent and credible radicalism was a response the depression called for, but the Socialists did not offer it.

The depression exposed Northeim's Socialists in other ways, too. The use of economic pressure at the sugar factory and at the railroad deprived the SPD of much of its prestige and power. If it could not even defend its own people when the chips were down, how could it defend democracy, and how could it bring about the socialist society? The success of management's action at the railroad yards no doubt opened up several possibilities for the Nazis. It was there that they learned how economically vulnerable the workers were; it was there that they learned essentially that the SPD would not fight.

But the main effect of the depression was to radicalize the town. In the face of the mounting economic crisis, Northeimers were willing to tolerate approaches that would have left them indignant or indifferent under other circumstances. Thus the disgusting and debilitating party acrimony and violence mushroomed in the years before the dictatorship. The extent of the violence in Northeim was an expression of the radical situation, but it also added to it by making violence normal and acceptable. Along with the growing nationalism and increasing impatience over the depression, violence and political tension were significant factors in preparing the town for the Nazi takeover.

All these factors were exploited with considerable astuteness by Nazi propaganda. In the face of the senseless round of political squabbling and fecklessness, the Nazis presented the appearance of a unified, purposeful, and vigorous alternative. Their propaganda played upon all the needs and fears of the town and directed itself to almost every potential group of adherents. This was largely because the Nazis were willing to be programmatically flexible in their propaganda and because they had a simple feedback system to measure and adjust the effectiveness of their propaganda. By their own energy, adaptability, and effort Northeim's Nazis captured the allegiance of the town's confused and troubled middle class.

This set the stage for the actual seizure of power, but the revolution itself was also conducted in such a way as to insure success. The fact that this was, in the words of Konrad Heiden, a *"coup d'état* by installments"* kept the *Reichsbanner* from responding decisively at any one point. By the time the SPD had been broken, the terror system had been inaugurated, largely through social reinforcement.

The single biggest factor in this process was the destruction of formal society in Northeim. What social cohesion there was in the town existed in the club life, and this was destroyed in the early months of Nazi rule. With their social organizations gone and with terror a reality, Northeimers were largely isolated from one another. This was true of the middle class but even more true of the workers, since by the destruction of the SPD and the unions the whole complex of social ties created by this super-club was effaced. By reducing the people of Northeim to unconnected social atoms, the Nazis could move the resulting mass in whatever direction they wished. The process was probably easier in Northeim than in most other places, since the town contained so many government employees. By virtue of their dependence on the government the civil servants were in an exposed position and had no choice but to work with the Nazis if they valued their livelihood. Especially Northeim's teachers — who formed the social and cultural elite of the town — found themselves drawn into support of the NSDAP almost immediately. As other Northeimers flocked to the Nazi bandwagon in the spring of 1933, and as terror and distrust became apparent, there was practically no possibility of resistance to Hitler.

T. W. Mason

Workers in the German Labor Front

The months after the physical destruction of the Trade Unions on 2 May 1933 were marked by chaos and confusion in the social and economic life of Germany, and, in the minds of all ruling groups — industrialists, civil servants and Party leaders alike — by the greatest uncertainty about the shape of the new social order. Gradually, in consequence of the terror and of bitter factional disputes among the ruling groups, the lines of development hardened: the verbose theorists of a "corporative social order" succumbed to the practitioners of Party supremacy; and the deep yearning of the rank and file Nazis to do away with large-scale industry altogether soon proved to be incompatible with the more pressing task of doing away with the Treaty of Versailles. Two new institutions and one old one emerged into an uneasy and mutually suspicious equilibrium to preserve, exhort and exploit the mutilated body of the German working classes.

The task of preservation was allotted to the state. Deprived of the protection of the independent trade unions and of the workshop councils, workers — especially those in smaller undertakings — were being forced in the spring and early summer of 1933 to agree to further wage reductions: there was a reserve labour army of seven million unemployed, and where the impersonal terror of starvation did not suffice, the SA had rawhide whips and rubber truncheons for the enlightenment of "marxists" who failed to recognize that 30 January had brought a new spirit of national and social unity. But the further immiseration of the working classes was not to the advantage of the new régime. In contrast to his straightforwardly reactionary supporters, Hitler recognized that he could not simply preside over the working population in an aloof, bureaucratic manner; the logic of mass politics demanded that he seek their active support. He claimed that he had liberated the working classes from the tyranny of their corrupt marxist "Bonzen", restored the dignity of manual labour and emancipated it from the deprecating glance of the brain-worker. Translated into material terms, these sentiments demanded the retention of existing minimum wage levels; to this end the new official post of Trustee of Labour was created. The Trustees were responsible to the Ministry of Labour for enforcing old, and issuing new minimum wage regulations within a defined geographical area.

The task of exhortation fell to the German Labour Front, a misshapen child of hectic improvization. It was called into existence to defeat the ambitions of Nazi trade unionists in the Party's Factory Cell Organization, who threatened to outgrow the political tutelage of the Party and establish monolithic and radical workers' unions; the new Labour Front was to be tied much more closely to the party leadership. Hitler's most slavish follower, Robert Ley, who had commanded the Action Committee for the destruction of the Free Trade Unions, became *both* supreme organizational manager of the party *and* leader of the Labour Front. Ley was at first surprised by his new appointment, but soon recognized that the one was a mere extension of the other, that it was but a small step from managing the affairs of the party to managing the minds of the working population. The link should ensure that the mass management of minds would be conducted on the basis of orthodox ideological principles. Ley's dual function symbolized the new unity of the German people, a unity embodied only in the organization of the

NSDAP: independent working class organizations of any political persuasion were both dangerous and superfluous. But the original conception of the Labour Front demanded that the mass management of minds be its *sole* task. Influential employers were scarcely less frightened by the potential power of an organization, membership of which was in practice compulsory for all industrial workers, than they were by the brutal populism of the Factory Cell Organization. With the full support of the Ministries of Economics and Labour, the employers wrung from Ley in November 1933 a declaration that the Labour Front "would *not* be the organ through which the material questions of workaday life would be decided, *not* the organ within which the natural differences of interest inside the productive community would be resolved". Ley, fighting simultaneously against authoritarian and populist critics of his new rôle, and lacking at this stage a clear picture of the future shape of his organization, had no option but to agree. The employers then dissolved their own class organizations and joined the Labour Front, which became therewith the official bearer of the doctrine that class conflict had been abolished. In its place was to grow that deep and genuine affective harmony of German working people from all walks of life which had so long been latent in society, but the realization of which had so long been frustrated by the machinations of paid agents of Moscow. Affective harmony was good for productivity, and high productivity was both the proof and the goal of "German socialism". The social history of the next six years is the story of the bankruptcy of this ideal, at once cynical and sentimental, archaic and dilettantish. . . .

The activities of the Labour Front could be confined to propaganda only as long as this body was inchoate. By the autumn of 1934 this phase was past. In October of that year Ley obtained Hitler's signature to a "Decree on the Essence and Goals of the German Labour Front", which empowered it to secure "on the basis of National Socialist principles, a compromise between the just interests of all those involved in economic life". The legal status of the decree was disputed since neither Schacht (Minister of Economics) nor Hess (Minister for Party Affairs) had been consulted; Cabinet approval was necessary for any decree modifying the Law for the Organization of National Labour. Hitler, however, saw no reason to clarify the situation. At a local level too, the Labour Front was showing scant respect for legal formalities. Towards the end of October 1934, Graf von der Goltz, Deputy Leader of the Economy, reported in the following terms to the Reich Chancellory on its activities:

> Its functionaries have arrogated to themselves the power to inspect factories at any time, to examine the possibility of improving their social amenities, to negotiate on hours of work and wages, and to investigate every complaint. The brown uniform, the authority of the Party and occasionally, if necessary, the threat of physical violence usually suffice to browbeat small employers into making any concession. Complaints are rare since employers fear reprisals, and have little confidence in the power of the Trustees of Labour. The task of the Labour Front to give retinues an understanding of the problems of their factories will lead to a continuation of the endless questionnaires about raw materials, production costs, etc., with which the Labour Front has been bombarding the plants. . . . the foundation of the Law for the Organization of National Labour was the immediate settlement of all problems within the plant community by the leader, Council of Trust and the retinue. This foundation has been deserted. . . . It must be openly stated that these developments portend the danger of an immensely dynamic trade union . . . .

In the light of what later happened, the report seems a little alarmist and backward-looking. This type of insubordinate activity hardly affected larger firms, and was combated elsewhere with some success by the Ministry of Economics. Neither does the comparison with a trade union bear closer inspection. Ley spoke often of "soldiers of labour", and the relationship between Labour Front functionary and worker was similar to that between NCO and private: the private could not elect a new sergeant, and the private's welfare was for the sergeant a subordinate consideration in the pursuit of goals determined for him by the General Staff. Basically however, von der Goltz was right; if the Labour Front, which had a full-time paid staff of 30,000 and a revenue roughly twice as large as that of the party, was to have the task of converting the working classes to National Socialist doctrines, it could not be restrained from intervention in material matters of direct concern to the working class.

The precise nature of these material matters was defined not by the working class itself, but by the mammonistic anti-materialism of Nazi social ideas. Beauty and joy became the rhetorical organizing principles of industrial society; sordid and contentious haggling over Pfennigs per shift was a thing of the inglorious past, and fringe benefits were restored to their proper central position in the social world. Work was a creative, joyous experience, and a happy labour force was a productive labour force; happiness could be engendered by those employers with the necessary resources to take seriously their legal duty to care for the welfare of their retinues. The Labour Front department "Beauty of Work", run by a young architect called Albert Speer, persuaded employers that they had a moral obligation to improve the productivity of their retinues by beautifying their factories and improving their social amenities. By 1940 "Beauty of Work" had been instrumental in the re-decoration of 26,000 workshops, the provision of 24,000 washing and changing rooms and 18,000 canteens and rest-rooms, the laying out of 17,000 gardens in industrial plants, and the building of 3,000 factory sports grounds.

The Factory Inspectors reported with disquiet the anti-social behaviour of workers who had to be warned for refusing to make use of such new facilities, and persisted in eating their sandwiches brought from home on an upturned orange-box beside their lathe. Even more anti-social were those workers who defaced and damaged new installations, treating the tiled showerbaths like the old huts which they had always been used to. "Clean men in a clean factory!", "Join the fight against noise!", "Good lighting means good work!", "Everyone contributes to the shaping of his factory!", "Happiness at the bench means higher productivity!" But some were slow to see where their own best interests really lay, and it took the guile of the industrial architect, the frantic incessant gaiety of Labour Front slogans and the fear of the Gestapo to enlist them in the joyful preparations of total war.

No less dissimilar from the standard activities of a trade union was the Labour Front's sponsorship of a national scheme for cheap holidays and entertainment. "Strength through Joy" was conceived by the Party leadership late in 1933, and its potential appeal was tested empirically by the personnel management of the Siemens Electrical Company in Berlin in the spring of 1934. A questionnaire compiled with the advice of the Berlin *Gauwart* of "Strength through Joy" and distributed to all of Siemens' 42,000 workers, showed "how small is the circle of those who carry forward the cultural and physical existence of a nation". Only 6,500 workers went to the theatre more than twice a year, and only 7,500 to the cinema more than twice a month; only 8,000 bought more than three books a year, and 28,500 never travelled outside the

Berlin area; only 3,500 were members of a Sports Club, and of the men, less than one sixth were members of para-military formations. The facilities were available, and, as the existence of 14,000 amateur photographers proved, it was not just material poverty which kept the élite so narrow. . . .

The German countryside and German culture were translated by a gigantic feat of organization into commodities to which all Germans should have equal access: symphony orchestras played in the factories during the lunch-hour, and firms were given cheap block-bookings for the civic theatres at night; factory libraries were expanded (and purged), sport was nationally organized, encouraged and subsidized so that even the poorest unskilled worker was able to sail or play tennis; and folk-culture groups revived and performed traditional rural songs and dances. Early in 1934 the loudspeakers in the Berlin factories blared out the news of the arrival of the first train-load of "Strength through Joy" holiday-makers in Bavaria. The expansion was swift, and within months the press was carrying photographs of happy German tourists in Madeira and Lisbon and in the Norwegian fjords, transported in passenger ships converted to double the number of available berths. National Socialism had achieved one of the great aims of the International and had laid Europe at the feet of the German worker. Lest he abuse the privilege, the German worker was accompanied on his foreign tours by well-deserving old Gestapo officers, who saw that he did not contact subversive exile organizations.

If Joy could be produced by economies of scale in the tourist industry it was not for its own sake, nor even for the greater glory of the Third Reich. Joy was an essential condition for recuperating from the trials and strains of industrial labour, for re-conditioning the mind and the body for yet more intensive efforts in the battle for production. But many remained oblivious of this higher purpose of the political fun-palace, and gave themselves over hopelessly to the simple pursuit of pleasure. In 1938 Ley had to remind passengers on a "Strength through Joy" cruise that the organization did not exist to lay on orgies, and in the country at large it was whispered ironically that many a girl had lost her strength through a surfeit of joy. . . .

The first signs of crisis in the labour market came in the summer of 1935, when the spate of military and civil building in North Germany made it very difficult for employers to find the necessary workers; worst affected were building sites in rural areas, where autobahns and barracks

The End of the Thousand-Year Reich. In Hitler's grand plan, Germany's capital city was to have been the center of the world for centuries to come. Instead, after intensive bombing by the Allies, it offered a picture of haunting devastation. (UPI/Bettmann Newsphotos)

were being built. Wage rates were calculated according to a cost of living index, and in rural areas food was much cheaper and wages appreciably lower. The Ministry of Labour at once proposed a measure of equalization, whereby rural wage rates should be increased and inflated urban rates reduced. At the insistence of Party officials, notably Gauleiter Kaufmann of Hamburg, the proposal was vetoed by Hitler, on the grounds that it was impossible to *reduce any* wage rates so soon after the great unemployment, *and* to hope to make progress with the task of gaining the political loyalty of the working class. A fateful pattern was taking shape: the régime needed the political approval of the working classes and their full co-operation in the armaments drive, but the fewer unemployed there were, the less necessary it became for the working classes to give their full cooperation; and this political weakness of the régime for a long time inhibited measures which could have remedied the economic weakness. Hitler constantly asserted the primacy of politics over economics; by March 1942 this meant the primacy of terror. What it was politically impossible, but economically essential to demand of the German working classes, could be demanded without scruple of sub-human slave labour, transported in cattle trucks into the Reich from Eastern Europe.

In the summer of 1935 this fulfillment was a long way off, but in the following twelve months the cycle advanced by several steps. When Goering was charged by Hitler in September 1936 to carry out a Four Year Plan which should make the German economy ready for war by the time of its completion, he found signs of strain throughout the labour market. . . .

In the spring of 1938 the crises came to a head. The unpublished wage statistics kept by the Ministry of Labour show that hourly money earnings increased on average by 5.5% between December 1935 and June 1938, average weekly earnings by 8.2% over the same period, the difference derived from longer hours of work. In the first quarter of 1938, hourly earnings began to increase much more rapidly than weekly earnings. The statistics scarcely did justice to the dimensions of the problem. The wage spiral was uncontrolled and very unevenly spread: many textile workers were still receiving the same hourly wages as in 1932 for a shortened working week, and similar conditions prevailed in most consumer goods industries. The real beneficiaries of the labour shortage were that 35% of the employed population who worked in the iron, metals and building industries. It was precisely those branches of the economy most vital to the rearmament programme which were most severely affected. Further, the wage spiral developed at a time when foreign, military and economic policy conspired to demand a *reduction* in consumer expenditure, and a heightened concentration of national resources on rearmament. And the wage statistics were silent on the high mobility of labour, falling productivity and the collapse of work-morale.

On 25 June 1938, in the shadow of the crisis over Czechoslovakia, Goering issued the Decree on Wage Formation, by which the Trustees of Labour were empowered to set maximum wage levels in branches of industry designated by the Ministry of Labour; employers breaking these regulations could be sentenced by the courts to unlimited fines or periods of imprisonment. The decisive step was taken, and from this point on the régime relied more and more on sheer administrative force to "solve the labour problem". Considerations of popularity were reluctantly jettisoned, and only the threat of war remained to justify these measures to the people whom they affected. Rearmament entailed a progressive militarization of working life; ideological militarization and the destruction of democratic controls had produced cynicism among wide sections of the population; in the summer of 1938 legal and physical militarization became necessary to make good the failure of this first policy — prescribed work at prescribed wage rate. Strategic policy and the shortage of raw materials were dragging a growing proportion of the labour force away from their homes, and housing them in wooden barracks in the middle of the North German plain or on the Westwall; the Labour Front and "Strength through Joy" catered for their welfare and entertainment. Up to June 1938 these men were free to leave this brutalized existence if they could find other work, but simultaneously with the Decree on Wage Formation, a Decree on the Duty of Service was issued, which empowered the government to conscript workers for tasks of exceptional state-political importance; employers could be forced to surrender a percentage of their labour force, and the workers, provided that they were physically fit, had to comply. Factory leaders used this opportunity to get rid of the most disaffected and "anti-social" elements in their retinues, who were then shipped off to the French frontier to build fortifications. 300,000 men were working under these conditions when Germany invaded Poland, over half of them on the Westwall. By a further decree of midsummer 1938, the firing of any worker or engineer by any firm in the building industry was made conditional on the approval of the local labour exchange. And at the same time, all convicts in German prisons were set to work for the armaments drive — among the convicts were some 8,000 metal workers.

These measures marked a fundamental change in attitude and policy on the part of the government, but their effects on the way of life of the working population were limited, and social and economic practice conformed only slowly, reluctantly and incompletely to the new spirit. The difficulties of deciding on maximum wage rates were great, and those of enforcing them still greater; the cutting back of inflated rates caused discontent and disruption, and, as Goering had noted in rejecting this solution in 1936, there was no plaintiff in a prosecution for the payment of illegally high wages. In the months after June 1938 the government repeatedly exhorted industry to observe the letter of the law. There seem to have been very few cases of employers being fined or imprisoned; wage increases were widely disguised in the form of free accommodation, the present of a life insurance premium, the payment of social insurance contributions, or, as in one particularly crude case, the gift of motorcycles. But these were wide loopholes in a slowly tightening net. The Trustees of Labour reported favourably on the short-term effects of the maximum-wage legislation: the hectic search for better paid jobs gradually died down, as did the disruptive pressure of the retinues for higher wages. Goering's fears of 1936 that such legislation would bring the authority of the state into discredit were probably not fully realized, but the measure did not and could not touch the main social problem: the stubborn, despairing refusal of the working classes to become the selfless servants of the régime. If the events of autumn 1939 are any guide, legal and physical militarization made this problem more, not less acute. Similarly, both the Decree on the Duty of Service and the Decree on the hiring of labour in the building industry proved inadequate for their respective tasks, and both had to be re-enacted in a more radical form in the spring of 1939; these attempts to restrict the mobility of labour were in some areas supplemented by the Trustees of Labour, who lengthened the minimum legal period of notice to up to three months.

The process of the full militarization of the labour force thus began slowly and uncertainly; and the old logic of the plebiscitarian system was not yet quite played out. In the late summer of 1938, shop assistants in North Germany flatly defied orders from the Ministry of Economics, and instituted early closing on Saturdays, oblivious to appeals that they should show solidarity with their overworked comrades in the armaments plants. The Labour Front weakly offered its retroactive blessing on this increase in the beauty and joy of the lives of the shop assistants; two months later, Goering vented his rage and frustration with the intractable economic problems on the Labour Front, threatening to clap its officials in gaol if they persisted in forcing employers to build swimming baths for their retinues.

The winter of 1938–9 brought no relief; the shortage of labour grew more intense and came to cover all degrees of skill in all trades. Firms had to be prevented by the government from depopulating Austria and the Sudetenland after the acquisition of those territories by the Reich, and unsuccessful attempts were made to mobilize young women for work in agriculture. In February 1939 a new Decree on the Duty of Service was necessary; that of June 1938 had promised to conscript only unmarried men, to pay them at least the same wages as they were already earning, and to conscript them for a limited period of time. No such promises were made by the new decree. In the following month, the controls over the hiring of building workers were extended to cover the hiring and firing of all workers in all major industries: agriculture, chemicals, building materials, iron, steel, metal-working and mining. The prior consent of the labour exchange had to be obtained in every case. A general and complete direction of labour was begun, designed to ensure that the priority tasks of rearmament could be carried out. But the social and economic reality still proved recalcitrant. No clear system of economic priorities was worked out in peace-time; the priority list was supplemented by a super-priority list, which was in turn made obsolete by the internecine rivalry among the armaments firms and among the three branches of the armed forces. Scarcity turned the ideology of ruthless struggle into a set of maxims of prudence for the conduct of everyday life in the Third Reich. Of equal importance for the operation of the latter decree was the fact that the labour exchanges, themselves short of trained staff, could not really cope with their new duties. Clear and generally applicable criteria for deciding whether a request to change jobs was justified or not, were extremely difficult to establish; decisions were erratic and varied from town to town. When applications from workers were refused, only the Gestapo could deal with those who showed their resentment at the decision by slacking — and the Gestapo could not *replace* these workers. The factory community, still invoked by the labour lawyers and the managers of minds, had become a brutal parody of the grim charade it once had been.

On the day the German army marched into Poland, the hiring and firing of all workers was made dependent upon the approval of the labour exchanges; offenders against this decree could be fined and/or imprisoned. For male workers over eighteen years of age, all legislation limiting hours of work was annulled, and the limitations on the hours of work of women and young persons were greatly loosened. Three days later, on 4 September 1939, a War Economy Decree empowered the Trustees of Labour to fix maximum wages *and working conditions* in all branches of industry: the piracy of skilled workers through the offer of generous fringe benefits now became illegal. Higher rates of pay for overtime work, Sunday-, holiday- and night-work were abolished: until the invasion of Poland it was standard practice in German industry for workers to receive time-and-a quarter for hours worked in excess of eight per day: now, in order that retinues should not think their leaders to be profiting unduly from the war, and in order that the burden of war finance for the government be eased, employers had to pay to the tax offices the difference between the standard and the overtime wage rates. Thus an eleven-hour day at a standard rate of I Rm. per hour brought the worker II Rm., and the tax office 75 Pf. It was, as Goebbels insisted, a people's war. And all regulations granting statutory holidays were suspended. The Trustees were exempted from having to prosecute offenders in the courts, and gained the power to fine them on the spot. The establishment of maximum wages and working conditions for the whole economy evidently proved much too cumbersome a task, and on 12 October, all wages were simply frozen. The suspension of holidays excepted, there is no indication that these desperate measures were considered temporary; the full weight of the intricate machinery of state was brought directly and suddenly to bear upon the working population.

Detlev Peukert

Obedient and Dissident Youth

National Socialist youth policy aimed to secure the younger generation's total loyalty to the regime and their willingness to fight in the war that lay ahead. All competitors had to be eliminated and Nazi forms of organisation and militaristic education developed. These tasks were to be achieved with the distinctively Nazi combination of compulsion and prohibitions on the one hand and incentives and enticements on the other.

In practice, contradictions arose between these objectives of youth policy, and particularly between the different methods of realising them: contradictions which fragmented and obstructed what appeared at first sight to be a uniform programme of totalitarian assimilation. For example, military conscription robbed the Hitler Youth of many badly needed older youth leaders. Competition between the rival authorities of school and the Hitler Youth gave rise to areas of conflict in which young people could play the one off against the other. And, not least, the ideological content of National Socialism remained much too vague. Fragmentary notions of racial and national arrogance were mixed up with traditional pedagogic humanism: the model of the front-line soldier mixed up with the idea that there was an especially profound and valuable "German" culture; backward-looking agrarian Romanticism mixed up with enthusiasm for modern technology.

The life stories of young people under the swastika often contain the most contradictory impressions. If there was any common denominator, it was an education in the reckless, ruthless pursuit of genuine or inculcated interests. The following extract hints at how this came about:

> No one in our class ever read Mein Kampf. I myself only took quotations from the book. On the whole we didn't know much about Nazi ideology. Even anti-Semitism was brought in rather marginally at school — for example via Richard Wagner's essay 'The Jews in Music' — and outside school the display copies of Der Stürmer made the idea questionable, if anything . . . . Nevertheless, we were politically programmed: to obey orders, to cultivate the soldierly "virtue" of standing to attention and saying "Yes, Sir," and to stop thinking when the magic word 'Fatherland' was uttered and Germany's honour and greatness were mentioned.

War seemed "normal"; violence seemed "legitimate." Hitler's foreign policy achievements between 1936 and 1939 had accustomed the Germans to regard the combination of violent posturing, assertion of their "legal right" to wipe out the "shame of Versailles," and risk-taking as a recipe for success.

The main arm of National Socialist youth policy was the Hitler Youth. By the end of 1933 all youth organisations, apart from the Catholic ones (which for the time being remained protected owing to the Nazi government's Concordat with the Vatican), had been either banned (like the socialist youth movement) or "co-ordinated" more or less voluntarily and integrated into the Hitler Youth (like the non-political *bündisch* youth movement and, in late 1933/early 1934, the Protestant organisations).

By the end of 1933, therefore, the Hitler Youth already contained 47 per cent of boys aged between ten and fourteen (in the *Deutsches*

Jungvolk) and 38 per cent of boys between fourteen and eighteen (in the Hitler Youth proper). However, only 15 per cent of girls between ten and fourteen were organised (in the *Jungmädelbund* and only 8 per cent of those between fifteen and twenty-one (in the *Bund Deutscher Mädel*). The Hitler Youth Law of December 1st, 1936, called for the incorporation of all German youth, and this was backed up with growing pressure on those remaining outside to enroll "voluntarily" — until two executive orders ancillary to the Hitler Youth Law, issued on March 25th, 1939, made "youth service" compulsory.

In the years immediately following 1933, many did not regard membership in the Hitler Youth as compulsory. The Hitler Youth built upon many practices of the youth organisations of the Weimar period, offered a wide range of leisure activities, and, at the lower levels (which in the everyday running of things were the most important), was led not infrequently by people who had had previous experience in other youth organisations. In addition, the Hitler Youth uniform often provided the chance to engage, sometimes quite aggressively, in conflict with traditional figures of authority: the teacher, the father, the foreman, the local clergyman.

For many young people in the provinces, where the youth movement was not widespread before 1933, the arrival of the Hitler Youth often meant the first access to the leisure activities in a youth organisation, the impetus to build a youth club or sports field, or the opportunity to go on weekend or holiday trips away from one's narrow home environment.

The emancipatory openings for girls were even greater. In the *Bund Deutscher Mädel* girls could escape from the female role-model centered around family and children — a role-model which, for that matter, was also propagated by the National Socialists. They could pursue activities which were otherwise reserved for boys; and if they worked as functionaries for the *Bund Deutscher Mädel* they might even approach the classic "masculine" type of the political organiser who was never at home. Such opportunities remained limited, however, and were withdrawn increasingly owing to the Nazis' general discrimination against women. Yet these groups undoubtedly proved, in many practical day-to-day respects, to be a modernising force.

With the consolidation of the Hitler Youth as a large-scale bureaucratic organisation, and with the gradual ageing of its leadership cadres in the course of the 1930s, the movement's attraction to the young people began to decline. Political campaigns within the Hitler Youth against those who had been leaders in the Weimar youth movement and against styles and behavior allegedly associated with that organisation led to the disciplining and purging of units. The campaign to bring everyone into the Hitler Youth ranks brought in those who previously had proclaimed their antipathy simply by their absence. Disciplinary and surveillance measures to enforce "youth service" made even harmless everyday pleasures such as meetings of friends and cliques criminal offences. Above all, the claim of legal power by Hitler Youth patrols, whose members were scarcely older than the young people they were keeping track of, provoked general indignation. And in addition, even before the outbreak of war, the Hitler Youth concentrated increasingly on premilitary drill.

The belief that the Hitler Youth successfully mobilised young people is only half the story. The more the Hitler Youth arrogated state powers to itself and the more completely it drew young people into its organisation, the more obvious became the examples of deviant behaviour among adolescents. By the end of the 1930s thousands of young people were turning away from the leisure activities of the Hitler Youth and finding their own unregimented style in independent gangs. Indeed, they defended their independence all the more insistently as Hitler Youth patrols and the Gestapo increased their pressure. In 1942 the Reich Youth Leadership had to admit:

> *The formation of cliques, i.e. groupings of young people outside the Hitler Youth, has been on the increase before and, particularly, during the war to such a degree that one must speak of a serious risk of the political, moral and criminal subversion of youth.*

The leadership could not now make the excuse that the people involved had been conditioned by the Weimar "system": by "Marxism," "clericalism" or the old youth movements. The adolescents who made up this opposition in the late 1930s and early 1940s were the very generation on whom Adolf Hitler's system had operated unhindered.

Amidst the wealth of evidence of unaccommodating behaviour, two groups stand out particularly clearly, groups which shared a rejection of the Hitler Youth but which differed in their styles, backgrounds and actions: the "Edelweiss Pirates" (*Edelweisspiraten*) and the "Swing Youth" (*Swing-Jugend*).

The first Edelweiss Pirates appeared at the end of the 1930s in western Germany. The names of the individual groups, their badges (metal edelweiss flowers worn on the collar, the skull and crossbones, pins with coloured heads), their dress (usually a checked shirt, dark short trousers, white socks) and their activities all varied, but were based upon a single underlying model. "Roving Dudes" from Essen, "Kittelbach Pirates" from Oberhausen or Düsseldorf (named after a stream in the north of Düsseldorf) and "Navajos" from Cologne all regarded themselves as "Edelweiss Pirate" groups. This agreement took on real meaning during weekends trips into the surrounding countryside, where groups from the whole region met up, pitched tents, sang, talked, and together "bashed" Hitler Youth patrols doing their rounds.

The opposition — the Hitler Youth, Gestapo and the law — also soon categorised the groups under a single heading, having first wavered in case the "youth movement" (*bündisch*) label would save them the bother of having to analyse new, spontaneous forms of oppositional activity and construct corresponding new sets of prohibitions. It soon became clear, however, that although it was possible to spot precursor groups and so-called "wild" *bündisch* organisations in the early 1930s, there was no continuity of personnel (the "delinquents" of 1935–7 long since had been conscripted to the front) and there was no direct ideological line of descent.

The Edelweiss Pirate groups arose spontaneously, as young people aged between fourteen and eighteen got together to make the most of their free time away from the control of the Hitler Youth. The age composition of the group, with a clustering around it of younger children and older war-wounded men and women in reserved occupations, was not fortuitous: boys of seventeen and eighteen were conscripted into the National Labour Service and then into the Wehrmacht, while at fourteen boys reached the school-leaving age and could thus escape from the immediate, day-to-day sphere of Hitler Youth control. They were taking their first steps into work — as apprentices or, thanks to the shortage of manpower caused by the war, increasingly as relatively well-paid unskilled workers. To an increased sense of self-esteem and independence the continuing obligation of Hitler Youth service up to the age of eighteen could contribute very little. The war reduced the Hitler Youth's leisure attractions: instead there was repeated paramilitary drill with pointless exercises in obedience, which were all the more irksome for being supervised by Hitler Youth leaders scarcely any older than the rank and file, yet who often stood out by the virtue of their grammar or secondary-school background. "It's the Hitler Youth's own fault," one Edelweiss Pirate from Düsseldorf said, explaining his group's slogan "Eternal war on the Hitler Youth": "every order I was given contained a threat."

The self-confidence of the Edelweiss Pirates and their image among their peers were unmistakable, as an Oberhausen mining instructor found in the case of his trainees in 1941:

> *Every child knows who the KP [common abbreviation for Kittelbach Pirates] are. They are everywhere; there are more of them than there are Hitler Youth. And they all know each other, they stick close together . . . They beat up the patrols, because there are so many of them. They don't agree with anything. They don't go to work either, they're always down by the canal, at the lock.*

The overriding factor common to these groups was the territorial principle: they belonged together because they lived or worked together; and a gang usually consisted of about a dozen boys and a few girls. The fact that girls were involved at all distinguished these oppositional groups from the strictly segregated *Bund Deutscher Mädel* and Hitler Youth. The presence of girls at the evening get-togethers and on the weekend trips into the countryside gave the adolescents a relatively unrestricted opportunity to have sexual experiences. In this respect they were much less prudish than their parents' generation, particularly the representatives of Nazi organisations with their almost obsessive fixation on the repression of sexuality. Nevertheless, sexual life in these groups was no doubt much less orgiastic than contemporary authors of official reports believed, or wanted others to believe, when they sought to construct a trinity of delinquency out of (sexual and criminal) degeneracy, (anti-organisational and anti-authoritarian) rebellion, and (political) opposition.

The high point of the pirates' free time was the weekend, when the young people could go off on hikes. Armed with rucksacks, sheath knives and bread-and-butter rations, sleeping in tents or barns, they spent a carefree time with like-minded young people from other towns — although always on the watch for Hitler Youth patrols, whom they, prudently calculating their own strength, either sought to avoid or taunted and fell upon with relish.

An important reason for this need to get as much space as possible as often as possible between themselves and their everyday conditions was the wish to avoid the 'educative' incursions of adults and the daily experiences of denunciations, spying, orders and punishments by National Socialist institutions that were directly bound up with these incursions. The youth movement's old reason for hiking — to withdraw from the pressures of the adult world — was intensified and given a political dimension in the Third Reich. . . .

A quite different form of popular culture developed among young people from the upper middle class: the "Swing" movement. Its adherents took every opportunity to avoid *völkische* music and the "moon-in-June" triviality of German hit tunes in order to listen to jazz and swing numbers, either on records or with live bands. Initially some of these events were allowed to take place in public; then, when Hitler Youth officials took offence at them, they were banned. In one internal Hitler Youth report about a swing festival in Hamburg in February 1940, which was attended by 500–600 adolescents, one can hear all the leitmotifs that pervade the lamentations of authorities faced by the jazz and rock cultures of the twentieth century:

> *The dance music was all English and American. Only swing dancing and jitterbugging took place. At the entrance to the hall stood a notice on which the words "Swing prohibited" had been altered to "Swing requested." Without exception the participants accompanied the dances and songs by singing the English lyrics. Indeed, throughout the evening they attempted to speak only English; and some tables even French.*
>
> *The dancers made an appalling sight. None of the couples danced normally; there was only swing of the worst sort. Sometimes two boys danced with one girl; sometimes several couples formed a circle, linking arms and jumping, slapping hands, even rubbing the backs of their heads together; and then, bent double, with the top half of the body hanging loosely down, long hair flopping into the face, they dragged themselves round practically on their knees. When the band played a rumba, the dancers went into wild ecstasy. They all leaped around and mumbled the chorus in English. The band played wilder and wilder numbers; none of the players was sitting any longer, they all "jitterbugged" on the stage like wild animals. Frequently boys could be observed dancing together, without exception with two cigarettes in the mouth, one in each corner . . .*

With the ban on public functions, the swing movement shifted to informal groupings where, naturally, its character became more sharply defined. Swing clubs sprang up particularly in big cities: Hamburg,

Kiel, Berlin, Stuttgart, Frankfurt, Dresden, Halle and Karlsruhe. Their members were predominantly middle-class adolescents with enough schooling to be able to use the English lyrics and bits of foreign slang. Like the Edelweiss Pirates, who had used German-language hits against the National Socialists, so the *Swing-Jugend* picked up mainstream jazz that was quite permissible in variety shows and dances and radicalised it: they made in into an emblem of a youth culture that rejected the Hitler-Youth ideals, stripped it of its domesticated dance-floor character and favoured hotter varieties of what in Nazi parlance was termed "negro music." Dance music gave way to hot jazz; steps as learned in dancing classes gave way to free, spontaneous rhythmic movement, erect posture and tidy dress gave way to "jitterbugging," hair "down to the collar" (to quote the same Hitler-Youth report) and a cult of "slovenliness" and "sleaziness."

The characteristics of the swing scene reflected the difference in social background between the offspring of the urban middle class and the working-class Edelweiss Pirates. The latter met on street corners and in parks, outside the confines of the parental home yet within a neighbourhood territory. The swing boys and girls had the money, clothes and status to be seen at bourgeois city-centre night clubs, as well as homes that were large enough for them to indulge in their "jitterbugging" and "sleaziness" when their elders were out. They had gramophone records; they could get hold of chic English-looking clothes.

A relaxed regime in their parents' houses, or lack of nighttime supervision offered ample opportunity for gaining sexual experience. Reporting about the swing groups, the Nazi authorities stressed the incidence of promiscuity, group sex, sexual intercourse involving minors and, above all, unabashed pleasure in sexuality which was denounced as moral degeneracy. The wording and tone of such internal reports as a rule said more about their authors and readers than about the actual behaviour of the adolescents. Things were taken too literally that perhaps were only bragging; isolated "incidents" were generalised. Even this caveat, however, does not alter the fact that the sexual behaviour of these adolescents clearly deviated from National Socialist acceptability.

The swing youth were not anti-fascist in a political sense — their behaviour was indeed emphatically anti-political — but both Nazi slogans and traditional nationalism were of profound indifference to them. They sought their counter-identity in what they saw as the "slovenly" culture of the wartime enemies, England and America. They accepted Jews and "half-Jews" into their groups — another outrage for the Nazis — and gave ovations to visiting bands from Belgium and Holland.

The very disgust shown by the authors of the Nazi reports and their dramatisation of events indicate that Nazi officialdom felt attacked at the heart of its concept of itself and of the State. This is the only way, too, to explain the reaction of Heinrich Himmler, who wanted to put the "ringleaders" of the swing movement into concentration camps for at least two or three years of beatings, punitive drill and forced labour.

These alternative forms of social behavior within the Third Reich show that considerable sections of the younger generation held themselves aloof from National Socialism. When the Hitler Youth seemed to have established itself officially, with compulsory membership, it met with apathy and rejection on the part of many adolescents, who were constantly to be found along the border line between passive and active insubordination. Despite various forms of repression, opposition groupings seem also to have been attractive to many adolescents who did not actually join them.

Furthermore, the everyday experience of National Socialism, for both working-class and middle-class youth, and their need to give expression to their identity, ran so contrary to what National Socialist ideology and its encrusted organisational structures had to offer, that the creation by young people of their own cultural identity and alternative styles naturally made itself apparent above all in the realm that was important for their age group: namely, leisure. These subcultures demonstrated that National Socialism, even after years in power, still did not have a complete grip on German society: indeed, sections of society slipped increasingly from its grasp the more it was able to perfect its formal means of organisation and repression.

The two central projects of National Socialist social policy — the abolition of class division through feelings of belonging to a "racial community" (*Volksgemeinschaft*) and the smashing of the perceived threat to traditional values from modernity and internationalism — seem to have run aground even before the end of the Third Reich loomed ahead with military defeat.

National Socialism unintentionally paved the way for these manifestations of modern youth culture. Its power was sufficient largely to destroy the traditional forms of working-class and middle-class cultures. In their places, however, National Socialism could offer only military discipline, an anachronistic ideology and a stifling bureaucracy. The National Socialist blueprint for a future order failed to shape society in its image.

Jill Stephenson

The Wary Response
of Women

The paradoxical character of the NSDAP, as a revolutionary force pledged to restore Germany to a mythical past from which it could develop towards an ideal present and future, attracted to it from 1919 those who wanted to return to the point where, they felt, Germany had taken a wrong turning. Unification in 1871 had been part of the "correct" development, as far as it had gone, but the ensuring rapid industrialisation had brought urbanisation and the politicisation of the working class by Marxist Social Democrats. It had also, by its insatiable demand for cheap and docile labour, brought large numbers of women into exhausting, dirty and even dangerous work which threatened the healthy development of the "race" by damaging and debilitating Germany's mothers. The massive increase in women's employment outside the home in the thirty or so years before the First World War had also, by this analysis, threatened family life in other ways, by diverting housewives and mothers from their essential duties in the home for much of their life. Women were too busy or too tired to learn how to run a home in an orderly way, to protect their own health as childbearers, and to care adequately for their children. Improved methods of birth control from the later nineteenth century had led women to try to mitigate their problems by restricting the size of their family — yet again, in the Nazi view, endangering the future of the "race." The quality of German life, too, was under threat, with women, "the guardians of German culture," distracted by work, political agitation and the growth of a consumer society from their alleged age-old function of cherishing the nation's distinctive songs, dances, costumes and crafts.

The Nazi revolution would restore women to the idyllic destiny from which they had been diverted before the First World War and which was, said the Nazis, deliberately derided by the Marxists, internationalists, liberals and feminists who seemed, in the post-war period, to have emerged as the victors from Germany's pre-war political and social conflicts. And if women had been deflected from their destiny — which was only the fulfillment of the instinctive aspirations of the female nature, it was said — even before the war, the experience of the war and the trauma of the revolutionary upheavals in a number of Germany's cities in 1918–19 convinced increasing numbers of men and women that the circumstances of post-war Germany would only intensify the distortion. The kind of changes that could be achieved to counteract modern evils through the new parliamentary system would do no more than tinker with the symptoms, for example, the "filth" that was given free rein in literature and drama by the lifting of censorship. Nothing less radical than a revolution — a *national* revolution, not a Marxist one — could bring Germany back to the path of "correct" development. This was what the Nazi Party was fighting for in the *Kampfzeit* (time of struggle, up to 1933). Axiomatically, women could not participate actively in the struggle, since allowing them to do so would be simply to follow the false example set by the Nazis' adversaries. One of the spectres that remained with Nazi activists for years was the horror of women's participation in the attempted revolution of 1918–19, and Rosa Luxemburg — although she was a victim rather than a perpetrator of violence — became a symbol of the evils threatening German society. Years later, she and others were remembered with fear and loathing as an example of what National Socialism was pledged to prevent.

These sentiments contributed to the development of what may cautiously be called the Nazi view of women's role in the nation and in the Party. As Hans Frank was to say, there were "as many 'National Socialisms' as there were leaders," and the variations on the theme of women's place were legion. But it is generally safe to say that in the Nazi view women were to be "wives, mothers and homemakers"; they were to play no part in public life, in the legislature, the executive, the judiciary or the armed forces. Hitler himself frequently expressed opposition to women's participation in politics, claiming that it sullied and demeaned the female nature, as he saw it. It was partly Hitler's personal attachment to the image of women as "mothers of the nation" which delayed and then vitiated the introduction of labour conscription for women during the Second World War, although in his *Götterdäm-merung* mentality early in 1945 he was prepared to see women enlisted as soldiers and sent to the front. While leading Nazis differed about the extent to which women should be employed outside the home and to which they could usefully contribute to the Party's campaigns, they generally accepted that from earliest childhood girls should be brought up to accept motherhood as their "natural calling," and that all other roles they might assume or functions they might exercise should be consistent with childbearing and child-rearing. Again, this preoccupation derived largely from increasing anxiety in Nazi and non-Nazi circles alike in the 1920s about Germany's falling birth-rate.

While growing numbers of men were drawn to National Socialism in the 1920s because of these ideas among others, there were women, too, who found the Nazis' traditionalist approach to women's role attractive. For them, it was enough to sympathise with and support the Party's "fighting menfolk," and although small numbers of women joined the new local branches of the NSDAP which sprang up all over the country from the mid-1920s, most pro-Nazi women regarded it as inconsistent with their own and the Party's view of women's role to join a political party. But there were, almost paradoxically, a number of women with distinctly feminist views who gravitated to National Socialism because of its anti-Marxism, its ultra-nationalist and racist aspect, or for local or family reasons. It is clear that they either ignored the Party's pronouncements about women's role or else refused to take them seriously. In the critical years between 1930 and 1933 the Party gave them plenty of encouragement in their self-delusion at a time when its leadership was hoping to make a favourable impact on the female voter in its bid for power the legal way. Gregor Strasser, the Party's organisational chief at this time until his unexpected resignation in December 1932, particularly seemed to welcome and encourage women's participation in election campaigns. And so women supporters of National Socialism in the 1920s, up to 1933, might or might not wholeheartedly support the Party's general view of women's place in society, and might or might not be members of the NSDAP.

Women's group activity developed something of a split personality because it embraced these different kinds of women. It also started and grew spontaneously and in a variety of forms because the inherent male chauvinism of the movement led to exclusive concentration on the men's struggle against the Weimar "system." Often enough, a woman whose husband or brother was a Party member would join in giving *ad hoc* support to the men in the area, providing food, making and mending uniforms, or, as in Hanover in 1922, for example, making a flag bearing the Party's symbol. These activities set the tone for what would throughout the rest of the Nazi era be known as "womanly work," the kind of mundane, practical assistance which women, as homemakers, could readily provide, and which men really could not be asked to contemplate. This division of labour reflected the Party's general view of women's functions and underlined its insistence on the segregation of the sexes at work and at play. Women's talents and capacities were different from men's, and, like men's, they should be utilised to the full and not squandered in vain attempts by women to take over men's work or emulate men's achievements. Because of initial neglect of women's contribution to the Party's work, which led to its growth independently of male control, this segregationist policy led perhaps not to "secondary racism," but certainly to organisational apartheid. The male chauvinist mentality of the NSDAP's men ensured that women who were attracted to the Party were condemned to "separate development," which allowed them to work out their role in the Party's service to a great degree as they chose.

The evolution of Nazi women's groups of different kinds caused problems for the Party once it belatedly acknowledged their existence and assistance, in the later 1920s. To solve these, Gregor Strasser ordered the dissolution of all existing women's groups in 1931 and created, in their stead, the NS-*Frauenschaft* (NSF — Nazi Women's Group), the first official Nazi women's organisation under central Party control. Strasser's role here and in the subsequent development of the NSF casts interesting light on his character and methods. Unlike many leading Nazis he clearly felt that the women's organisation could contribute usefully to the Party's work; this was no doubt why he was at pains to create a uniform, harmonious organisation out of the diverse warring factions which had evolved in the 1920s. Others, too, valued the "women's work." The SA depended on women's soup kitchens to feed its members when they were on duty, especially if they were unemployed, and for a time the SA welcomed the rudimentary first-aid service provided by Nazi women for "heroes" hurt in brawls. As the

Women for the Fatherland. This Nazi propaganda poster has a beaming young woman, wearing a soldier's helmet, standing bravely at her antiaircraft post. In reality women were relegated to the kitchen, the nursery, or the factory, where they were expected to perform menial tasks in a man's world. (Wide World Photos)

Depression hit Germany's larger towns particularly hard from 1930 onwards, welfare work by women who collected money, cast-off clothing and household utensils, who gave material and moral support to the families of political detainees, and who provided food and warm clothing for destitute Germans, whether they were Party supporters or not, was regarded as vital in both practical and propaganda terms.

As the Party's apparatus and ambitions grew, so it came to create new, permanent institutions to replace the voluntary, *ad hoc* work done by women enthusiasts. The SA in Berlin, for example, developed its own specialist medical corps and increasingly — and ungratefully — rejected the assistance which women's groups continued to provide. The founding of the Nazi welfare organisation (*NS-Volkswohlfahrt* — NSV) in Berlin in winter 1931–2 similarly led to a downgrading of the spontaneous assistance for long provided by women's groups. And in July 1932 the order that the Hitler Youth should have a monopoly of organising Nazi girls threatened to deprive the NSF of its traditional function of bringing the young into the movement, under the guidance of their elders. After tooth-and-nail resistance from the women, this order was enforced in 1933, but only by replacing the existing leadership in the NSF in the first of a series of changes which culminated in the appointment of Gertrud Scholtz-Klink as NSF leader in February 1934. By the time she took office, the women's organisation had been shorn of most of the functions it had exercised in the *Kampfzeit*, and in spite of official propaganda to boost its image it never recovered from these losses. The demarcation disputes in which the NSF became involved, with the NSV and the Hitler Youth especially, during the 1930s and into the war, were a reflection of the extent to which NSF leaders refused to be reconciled to those losses, and to which they recognised the damage they had inflicted on the NSF's authority and prestige. . . .

But if the Party and its women's groups were middle-class in orientation and appeal, this did not mean that all, or even most, middle-class women were attracted to them. There were enthusiasts, and there were also women who joined because they regarded membership as a useful insurance policy, particularly if they had a professional career to conserve. Often enough they merely paid their subscription and were classed, on investigation, as "inactive" members; it was a continuing source of frustration to NSF and Party officials that women from the "educated classes" generally held aloof from the women's organisation. And middle-class women were certainly not in the forefront of those responding to Party and NSF appeals for volunteers to help the German war-effort from 1939. Only a minority of women — in contrast with men — tends to favour single-sex group activity, and a single-sex monopoly organisation with a heavy emphasis on propaganda and indoctrination at once made itself unattractive to large numbers of women, whatever their class. Some women joined no doubt because they wanted to be members of a music group or sports club or sewing circle, and had to choose between the Nazi-sponsored one, under DFW control, or nothing. But, even so, German women were, contrary to the popular view, peculiarly resistant to National Socialism, and probably, because of their relative inaccessibility, much more resistant than men. And there was another reason: German women, like women elsewhere, remained more attached than men to religion. The spiritual authority of the Churches, particularly the Catholic Church in rural areas, retained the allegiance of large numbers of women in the face of competition from the NSF. It was hardly a contest: the Nazis could not hope to win against one of the traditional forces in society which many had believed they were coming to power to safeguard against "atheistic Marxism." Unable to use coercion to win recruits to the DFW, the NSF found, uncomfortably, that it was largely preaching to a converted minority, still cut off from the antagonistic or, more likely, uninterested 90 per cent and more of the female population of Germany.

Annexations before and during the war provided the Party and its affiliates with pastures new, with millions more ethnic Germans to Nazify. If this lifted morale, the effect was only temporary as the same problems emerged in the new territories as had dogged the NSDAP's efforts in the "old Reich." After a wave of initial enthusiasm by a susceptible minority, there remained the mass of the apathetic who, without necessarily being anti-Nazi, wished simply to remain private, unorganised citizens. And attempts to mobilise the organised for extra efforts in wartime revealed a disquieting amount of negativism among even them. It became increasingly clear that many of those who had joined the women's organisation had done so less out of burning enthusiasm for the Nazi cause than because they felt that self-interest would be served by belonging to the official women's organisation; most women of this disposition wanted not so much to be ordinary members as to hold an office or some kind. Favour and status, then, were the preoccupations of many who actually joined the DFW; it may be that the overwhelmingly middle-class character of the organisation determined this, with women who felt they had a position in society to maintain reluctant to be mere ordinary members — working members — of the DFW. The war highlighted the plight of the NSF and DFW by clearly showing up who were activists and who were passengers, and there was no doubt that the former were in the minority. They were left with the unpopular task of trying to maintain morale at home in the face of growing discomfort and the manifest injustice of the way in which the subject of labour conscription was treated by Hitler above all. The NSF's middle-class leaders were highly critical of how the system bore most heavily on working-class women, with large numbers of middle-class women managing to remain immune. The enthusiasts who were left to carry the burden of popular discontent obviously regarded themselves as the representatives of all German women, but government and Party policies had long since worked to deny them the chance to play this role in any way effectively.

It was perhaps fitting that the women's organisation should revert, towards its end, to something akin to what its predecessors had been in the 1920s, small local groups working in difficult circumstances to mitigate distress, this time among fellow citizens who were victims of air raids or the more or less willing subjects of evacuation policies. With shortages and the rupture of the communications' network towards the end of the war, the NSF's activities must have borne an uncanny resemblance to those of the *Kampfzeit*, with little or no central control of individual local policies. And it was clearly in emergency circumstances, in small groups of dedicated activists, that the Nazi women's work flourished. The extent of central authority effectively wielded by Gertrud Scholtz-Klink from her office in Berlin had always depended on the degree to which a Gauleiter had or had not intervened, but the chains of command in the women's organisation had been established at an early stage and had at least nominally held until well into the war. Their purpose had been to try to ensure that the work of the women's organisation throughout the country was conducted in a uniform way, to serve at the local level the demands of the regime as enunicated by the NSDAP and detailed by the staff of bureaucrats gathered in Gertrud Scholtz-Klink's central office. This contrasted sharply with Strasser's creation of the NSF in 1931 as essentially the women's branch of the Party, serving its needs at the local level. Strasser had himself set in motion the centripetal forces, which would ultimately and stultifyingly culminate in a top-heavy administrative centre whose edicts were intended to determine the nature of local women's group activity everywhere. But this conclusion was the logical one only to men, like his successors, with minds less flexible than his own. Unimaginative men with totalitarian aspirations produced a bureaucratic jungle in the women's organisation, as elsewhere; but here they were helped by their choice, as women's leader, of an equally unimaginative woman. No doubt the obsession with order and uniformity — which competing jurisdictions and a barrage of paperwork successfully vitiated — was yet another deterrent to potential recruits to the women's organisation at the local level. Those who joined up and stayed the course had as their reward a brief taste of initiative and freedom from the centrally-imposed straitjacket in the last months of the war, before the total eclipse.

Sarah Gordon

The Fate of German Jews

Jews represented only a small percentage of the German population in the period 1870–1933, but they were highly visible because of their concentration in large cities, in specific occupations (particularly trade, commerce, free professions, and cultural fields), in higher income brackets, and in political parties of the Middle and later the Left. This exposure made their numbers seem much greater than they were. Both German and immigrating Eastern European Jews attempted to reduce their specific differences from the population by abandoning their customs and even their religion, and through intermarriage. By 1933 Jews in Germany had achieved levels of integration that were indeed impressive, considering that large percentages of them were first-generation immigrants or recent migrants to new cities. Nevertheless, continuing objective differences between Jews and non-Jews made it easy to stereotype Jews as aliens who did not fit into German society. This was standard propaganda for anti-Semites between 1870 and 1945.

Many historians think that intellectual and social anti-Semitism

From Sarah Gordon, *Hitler, Germans and the "Jewish Question,"* Copyright © 1984 by Princeton University Press. Excerpt, pp. 296–306, (footnotes omitted) reprinted by permission of the publisher and the author.

increased during these years in response to the rise of the *"völkisch"* ideology, Social Darwinism, "social conservatism," nationalism, and imperialism. Still, some political parties were at least initially sympathetic to Jews and attempted to insure their fair treatment. Before 1928, parties whose major appeal was anti-Semitism were clearly an electoral failure; no major or minor rights of Jews were rescinded before Hitler came to power, despite the adoption of anti-Semitism around 1930 by some parties that had previously been neutral or sympathetic to Jews. Anti-Semitism does not appear to have been significant as an electoral issue for non-Nazi parties that advocated it sporadically before Hitler's election in 1933. . . .

Since extreme anti-Semitic propaganda often alienated potential voters, Hitler tempered his rhetoric after around 1925 and instead associated Jews with everything that the Nazis themselves disliked or what they assumed the population resented; however, he never outlined his concrete plans for the future treatment of Jews. Since Nazis associated Jews with every conceivable "evil" (internationalism, socialism, communism, parliamentary democracy, Germany's defeat in World War I, the Weimar system, finance capitalism, "interest bondage," reparations, the depression, etc.), the adjective "Jewish" served to focus resentment of these "evils" on a common enemy. This kept the appeal of anti-Semitism at a fairly abstract level of resentment and hostility, which undoubtedly relieved some of the tensions brought on by the depression and attendant political crises and helped to cement the heterogeneous elements within the Nazi party. Nevertheless, Nazi anti-Semitism per se does not appear to have been a major campaign issue except for a minority of voters.

Hitler developed an ethnic theory encompassing all of human history, which he defined as the struggle between nations for living space and world domination. He believed that Jews comprised a nation, albeit one spread out among other nations, and that they participated in the fight for world domination, but not for living space. In his ethnic theory all "subhumans" (including Poles and Russians) must be conquered and their leaders exterminated to prove the historical superiority of "Aryans." All Jews ("nonhuman parasites") must be exterminated because they occupied living space in the East and posed a racial "threat" to other nations, which Hitler thought they were attempting to overthrow from within. He actualized his ethnic theory in World War II when conquered "Aryan" nations were given special privileges, the

Systematic Segregation and Humiliation. A non-Jewish German woman and her Jewish boyfriend are forced to wear signs saying "I am the biggest pig in the place and have to do only with Jews" and "As a Jewish lad I only take German girls to my room." These epithets rhyme in German, but they bear the same meaning of shame as they do in English. (© Keystone/The Image Works)

leadership of "subhuman" nations was murdered, and most European Jews were exterminated.

His attitudes toward Jews also influenced domestic events in Germany before the war. All institutions and political parties that were "tainted" by "Jewish influence" were taken over and those that were suspected of opposing his racial and expansionist goals were purged.

Hitler's psychology was dominated by his misperceptions of the "Jewish threat" and his belief that Jews and all "Jewish inventions" must be "resisted" at all costs. His paranoia was clearly reflected in his ethnic theory, which accounts for his demonic destruction of millions of Jews. His murder of millions of non-Jews, however, did not result so much from paranoia as from his belief that "subhumans" who had been conquered in the past did not deserve anything better than enslavement and selective extermination.

Between 1933 and 1939 Hitler adopted a piecemeal policy to exclude Jews gradually from the political, economic, institutional, educational, social, and religious life of Germany. During the war he exterminated about 130,000 Jews who had remained in Germany and 30,000 who had emigrated to other parts of Europe, along with over five million other European Jews. It is argued here that despite Hitler's consideration of the effects of domestic and foreign opinion, including the attitudes of rabid anti-Semites within the Nazi party, he himself decided upon the timing of persecution and the extermination of Jews and others, because this was a logical consequence of his ethnic theory.

Hitler utilized anti-Semitism for several political purposes: to insure party unity by giving the party a role in racial policies, to dampen party criticism of his failure to implement the socioeconomic aspects of his program, to establish a new racial ideology, to terrorize the population and thus to atomize them socially, to divert Germans from his failure to effect a genuine social revolution, to weaken the power of "reactionaries" in the state bureaucracy, to justify expansion and war against other states that were allegedly dominated by Jews, and, finally, during the war, to include the SS, army, and bureaucracy as complicitors who would have to fight to the bitter end to prevent reprisals.

Anti-Semitic propaganda served many of the same functions, but its most important role was to create a consensus on anti-Semitism by spreading Nazi ideology and blacking out all facts or information about deportation and extermination, as well as other types of persecution, that would have led to questioning of that world view. As it became obvious that this attempt was only partly successful, tighter proscription of news and increased terror became necessary to ferret out real and potential opponents. This was most dramatically demonstrated after *Kristallnacht*, the burning of the synagogues and the general pogrom of November 1938, which was by and large a failure because ordinary Germans now widely questioned the morality and legality of the regime.

There were, of course, shifts in public attitudes toward the Nazi persecution of Jews, and these are reflected in general reports on public opinion. Certain types of measures, particularly legal or pseudo-legal exclusion of Jews from positions of prominence, authority, or economic power, appear to have been fairly well received, although some Germans attempted to aid individual Jews who were friends or neighbors. Before *Kristallnacht* even the Nuremberg Laws were acceptable to many, probably a majority, of Germans. However, the physical violence and brutality of *Kristallnacht* were clearly rejected by the same majority. Apparently anti-Semites and determined opponents of anti-Semitism were polarized around an indifferent or apathetic majority, yet one that was increasingly sympathetic to Jews during and after *Kristallnacht*. Public opinion reports indicate that widespread rumors of shootings in Poland and Russia were badly received by the public, which sometimes even attributed Germany's war losses to Hitler's rumored slaughter of Jews.

There are many possible reasons why so few Germans publicly protested these wholesale murders. Knowledge or even rumors of gassings, which were deliberately kept secret, were extremely rare outside of eastern Germany, so we have little information on German attitudes toward the death camps. Even though shootings of Russians, Poles, and Jews were widely rumored, their extensiveness was not grasped. Moreover, the rumors were apparently discounted as too fantastic to be believed; even if they had been believed, there was little that an individual or small groups of like-minded Germans could have done to halt the destruction. Only the churches and the army might have been able to interfere, and it is very doubtful that their intervention would have resulted in anything more than arrests and executions of protestors and their families. Thus an individual could act on his own, but he could not rely on higher institutions for additional support. . . .

In examining records of Germans who aided Jews it is seldom possible to determine their precise motivations, but a number of values appear to have been at play: patriotism, respect for law, order, and private property, conservatism, religious belief, socialism, and humanitarianism. Although some anti-Semites considered Jews to be totally alien foreigners who had never belonged in Germany in the first place and who had betrayed the country during World War I, some patriots, including Hindenburg, recognized that Jews had contributed to World War I both as leaders of great importance, such as Rathenau, and as front fighters. Moreover, many German Jews were well assimilated into German economic, political, social, and intellectual life; others had even converted and were religiously integrated. Significant numbers of Polish, Russian, and other Eastern European Jews had come to Germany, and they were not as well regarded either by Germans or German Jews. It is conceivable that those Germans who accepted German Jews would nevertheless have favored restrictions on immigration by

The Final Solution. A group of American senators visits the concentration camp at Buchenwald and witnesses the indescribable results of Nazi terror. In this case, surely, one picture is worth a thousand words. (UPI/Bettmann Newsphotos)

Eastern European Jews, yet this does not mean that they wanted to expel all Jews from Germany.

Another aspect of patriotism that may have played a role in opposition to Nazi racial policies was the significant contribution of Jews to German intellectual life. Not only had they brought honor to Germany by winning a large number of Nobel prizes, they were also very active in all scientific and cultural fields. Even Goebbels was slow to sever his ties with Jewish artists and performers who were considered first-rate in Germany. Jewish cosmopolitanism (which anti-Semites castigated as internationalism) also extended to their contacts with foreigners, primarily through trade, commerce, and banking. Germans who were not confirmed bigots could easily recognize the importance of Jewish entrepreneurship and international contacts for the German economy. Thus they did not necessarily perceive Jewish contacts abroad as treacherous.

Still another aspect of German patriotic values could also cut two ways. Although it became popular to excoriate "liberal" values after 1890–1900, not everyone believed they were evil. There was considerable diversity on this issue among the middle classes, and the lower classes (which represented almost 50 percent of the population) were in some ways more "liberal" than "socialist." Their complaint was that the "liberal" constitutional monarchy that Bismarck established, and which Jews supported strongly between 1871 and 1918, was not quite "liberal" enough.

In some ways Germany had been a pioneer in granting Jews rights and privileges. German universities had admitted Jews on an equal footing since 1790, and by 1909 and later they had a large percentage of Jewish professors when, for example, American and Canadian universities considered them anathema. Insofar as some Germans still believed the "liberal enlightenment" brought honor to the nation, and insofar as fair treatment of Jews was considered part of that enlightenment, some Germans viewed Hitler's attacks on Jews as a blight on national honor. Many of them equated Nazi violence against Jews with "primitive" countries and Bolshevik Russia. They complained that one might expect pogroms in "backward nations" such as Poland and Russia, but how could they happen in the land of Kant?

Closely related to the question of patriotism is the concept of a nation under law, because there can be no genuine national community without the assurance that laws will provide a stable political and economic order. In most societies law becomes a principle unto itself precisely for this reason. Germans have always had a healthy respect for a nation under law (a *Rechtsstaat*), and this is probably one reason the fall of the monarchy was a traumatic shock. The Weimar government had an entirely new legal foundation, one which challenged and changed past traditions and rights that had become ensconced in the law. The new state was a potential threat simply because it could and did change the law; therefore, it was viewed with fear. Some of this fear was quite rational, and some was hysterical; yet tampering with the monarchy and the old order could only have been expected to produce such fears.

When Hitler came to power, he made certain that his takeover had the appearance of legality; this was his craftiest political maneuver. It prevented the average German from perceiving that he would alter the entire legal system of Germany. Revolutionaries have never been popular in Germany, and Hitler would never have had the full aura of legitimacy he needed had he taken power by force. Accordingly, Nazi violence and illegality after Hitler became chancellor were widely condemned. Likewise, violence against Jews during the boycott of 1933, the summer riots in Berlin in 1935, and the pogrom of 1938 was condemned by many Germans on the traditional grounds that it violated the law. If the state itself authorized wanton illegality in one sphere, such as anti-Jewish measures, how could it maintain its image as defender of the laws in other spheres? Sporadic violent attacks on Jews before 1939 had to be curtailed because the public expected the state to perform its function of maintaining law and order. With the beginning of World War II and the attendant power it gave to Hitler, public indignation at violence against Jews in European lands could no longer have serious consequences. Germans who protested openly about persecution of Jews were treated as criminals because the traditional legal system was destroyed by Hitler, and his war powers could be terminated only with his death.

Suggestions for Additional Reading

Thousands of books and articles have been written about Nazi Germany. Few subjects in history have commanded so much scholarly attention. But here only a few titles can be listed, with apologies to the many worthy authors who are omitted. Nearly all of the works mentioned contain extensive bibliographies that can lead the reader further into monographs, memoirs, documentary materials, and general analyses in various languages. With one exception, only publications in English are included. The selected titles have been grouped into four parts corresponding to the structure of this anthology. Within these limits, this bibliography should provide a fairly comprehensive survey of recent scholarship on the Nazi era.

I The Nazi Movement and German History

Many textbooks have been devoted to Nazi Germany. Still reliable, albeit dated, is Koppel S. Pinson, *Modern Germany: Its History and Civilization*, rev. ed. (New York: Macmillan, 1966). Among more recent general accounts are William Carr, *A History of Germany 1815–1945*, 2d ed. (New York: St. Martin's Press, 1979); Volker Berghahn, *Modern Germany: Society, Economy, and Politics in the Twentieth Century*, 2d ed. (New York: Cambridge University Press, 1987); and Dietrich Orlow, *A History of Modern Germany, 1871 to Present* (Englewood Cliffs, NJ: Prentice-Hall, 1987). Debates about the continuity and unique course of German history already fill library shelves. It is advisable to begin with the two original versions represented in this anthology: Hans-Ulrich Wehler, *The German Empire, 1871–1918* (Leamington Spa, NH: Berg Publishers, 1985) and David Blackbourn and Geoff Eley, *The Peculiarities of German History* (New York: Oxford University Press, 1984).

The twin volumes by Arthur Rosenberg, *Imperial Germany: The Birth of the German Republic*, 3d ed. (Boston: Beacon Press, 1964) and *A History of the German Republic* (London: Methuen, 1936), are perceptive statements by a leftist historian deeply disappointed by the revolution of 1918. The insurrectionary events of that period, from which the Nazi movement emerged, are analyzed in the monographic works of Allan Mitchell, *Revolution in Bavaria, 1918–1919* (Princeton: Princeton University Press, 1965); A. J. Ryder, *The German Revolution of 1918* (Cambridge, England: Cambridge University Press, 1967); and F. L. Carsten, *Revolution in Central Europe, 1918–1919* (Berkeley: University of California Press, 1972). A brief but helpful survey of the interwar years is presented by A. J. Nicholls, *Weimar and the Rise of Hitler*, 2d ed. (New York: St. Martin's Press, 1979).

Local and regional histories have added significantly to our understanding of the rise of Nazism. Classic is the account of a small community by William Sheridan Allen, *The Nazi Seizure of Power: The Experience of a Single German Town, 1922–1945*, rev. ed. (New York: Franklin Watts, 1984). Nazi roots in Bavaria have been explored by Geoffrey Pridham, *Hitler's Rise to Power: The Nazi Movement in Bavaria, 1923–1933* (New York: Harper & Row, 1973) and Ian Kershaw, *Popular Opinion and Political Dissent in the Third Reich* (Oxford, England: Clarendon Press, 1983). Likewise, see Jeremy Noakes, *The Nazi Party in Lower Saxony, 1921–1933* (London: Oxford University Press, 1971); Johnpeter Horst Grill, *The Nazi Movement in Baden, 1920–1945* (Chapel Hill, NC: University of North Carolina Press, 1983); and on Marburg, Rudy Koshar, *Social Life, Local Politics, and Nazism* (Chapel Hill, NC: University of North Carolina Press, 1986).

The electoral appeal of Nazism is examined by Richard F. Hamilton, *Who Voted for Hitler?* (Princeton, NJ: Princeton University Press, 1982) and Thomas Childers, *The Nazi Voter: The Social Foundations of Fascism in Germany, 1919–1933* (Chapel Hill, NC: University of North Carolina Press, 1984). The composition of the party is considered by Peter Merkl, *The Making of a Stormtrooper* (Princeton, NJ: Princeton University Press, 1980) and Michael Kater, *The Nazi Party: A Social Profile of Members and Leaders, 1919–1945* (Cambridge, MA: Harvard University Press, 1983).

All in all, the best single general work remains that of Karl Dietrich Bracher, *The German Dictatorship: The Origins, Structure, and Effects of National Socialism* (New York: Holt, Rinehart and Winston, 1970).

II The Personality of the Leader

The standard biography of the Führer (and deservedly so) is by Alan Bullock, *Hitler: A Study in Tyranny*, rev. ed. (New York: Harper & Row, 1964), which is also available in an abridged edition. Another major attempt is that of Joachim C. Fest, *Hitler* (New York: Harcourt, Brace, and Jovanovich, 1974), which adds detail without offering a reinterpretation. Much briefer and full of interesting speculation is William Carr, *Hitler: A Study in Personality and Politics* (New York: St. Martin's Press, 1979). The early years are especially well handled by Bradley F. Smith, *Adolf Hitler: His Family, Childhood, and Youth* (Stanford, CA: Stanford University Press, 1967), which corrects Hitler's dramatization of his adolescence in *Mein Kampf* (available in several English editions). This theme is continued by Ian Kershaw, *The "Hitler Myth": Image and Reality in the Third Reich* (Oxford: Oxford University Press, 1987).

The first sensational episode of Nazi political history is related in extraordinary detail by Harold J. Gordon, *Hitler and the Beer Hall Putsch* (Princeton, NJ: Princeton University Press, 1972). Hitler's indispensability to his political movement is emphasized by Deitrich Orlow, *The History of the Nazi Party, 1919–1933*, 2 vols. (Pittsburgh: University of Pittsburgh Press, 1969–73); Martin Broszat, *German National Socialism, 1919–1945* (Santa Barbara, CA: Clio Press, 1966); and Joseph L. Nyomarkay, *Charisma and Factionalism in the Nazi Party* (Minneapolis: University of Minnesota Press, 1967).

An argument for the intellectual coherence of Nazism is maintained by Eberhard Jäckel, *Hitler's Weltanschauung: A Blueprint for Power* (Middletown, CT: Wesleyan University Press, 1972). But the irrational depths of Hitler's personality are plumbed by Robert G. L. Waite, *The Psychopathic God* (New York: Basic Books, 1977) and Rudolph Binion, *Hitler Among the Germans* (New York: Elsevier Press, 1976). The Führer's last folly is best described in the classic account of H. R. Trevor-Roper, *The Last Days of Hitler*, 3d ed. (New York: Berkeley Publishing Co., 1960).

III Industry, Church, and Army

Earlier works on the political role of industrial elites have been superseded by Henry Ashby Turner, Jr., *German Big Business and the Rise of*

Hitler (New York: Oxford University Press, 1985). Still useful, however, are Burton H. Klein, *Germany's Economic Preparation for War* (Cambridge, MA: Harvard University Press, 1959); Arthur Schweitzer, *Big Business in the Third Reich* (Bloomington, IN: Indiana University Press, 1964); and Alan S. Milward, *The German Economy at War* (London: Athlone Press, 1965). Milward has also published several monographs on the Nazi economic reorganization of occupied territories. Another analysis of note is by R. J. Overy, *The Nazi Economic Recovery, 1932–38* (London: Macmillan, 1982).

Three capable studies have concentrated on the role of Roman Catholicism in the Third Reich: Gordon C. Zahn, *German Catholics and Hitler's Wars* (New York: Sheed and Ward, 1962); Guenter Lewy, *The Catholic Church and Nazi Germany* (New York: McGraw-Hill, 1964); and John S. Conway, *The Nazi Persecution of the Churches* (New York: Basic Books, 1968). More broadly gauged, devoting equal attention to German Protestants, is Ernst Christian Helmreich, *The German Churches Under Hitler* (Detroit: Wayne State University Press, 1979).

Literature on the German military establishment is extensive and usually excellent. Three older studies treat the story up to 1933: Robert G. L. Waite, *Vanguard of Nazism: The Freecorps Movement in Postwar Germany, 1918–1923* (Cambridge, MA: Harvard University Press, 1952); Harold J. Gordon, *The Reichswehr and the German Republic, 1919–1926* (Princeton, NJ: Princeton University Press, 1957); and F. L. Carsten, *The Reichswehr and Politics, 1918–1933* (New York: Oxford University Press, 1966). That story of extended to the outbreak of war by Robert J. O'Neill, *The German Army and the Nazi Party, 1933–1939* (London: Cassell Press, 1966); E. M. Robertson, *Hitler's Pre-War Policy and Military Plans, 1933–1939* (New York: Citadel Press, 1967); and Wilhelm Diest, *The Wehrmacht and German Rearmament* (Toronto: University of Toronto Press, 1981). Spanning the entire period and harshly critical of the military caste are the pioneering works of John W. Wheeler-Bennett, *The Nemesis of Power: The German Army in Politics, 1918–1945* (London: Macmillan, 1953) and Gordon A. Craig, *The Politics of the Prussian Army, 1640–1945* (New York: Oxford University Press, 1956). A sociological profile of the subject is attempted by Karl Demeter, *The German Officer Corps in Society and State, 1650–1945* (New York: Praeger, 1965). The most notorious aspect of this topic is analyzed by Gerald Reitlinger, *The S.S. Alibi of a*

Nation, 1922–1945 (London: Heinemann, 1956); George H. Stein, *The Waffen SS: Hitler's Elite Guard at War, 1939–1945* (Ithaca, NY: Cornell University Press, 1966); and Heinz Höhne, *The Order of the Death's Head: The Story of Hitler's SS* (New York: Coward-McCann, 1970). These have been updated by Charles Sydnor, Jr., *Soldiers of Destruction: The SS Death's Head Division, 1933–1945* (Princeton, NJ: Princeton University Press, 1977). Among the many books to recount the eventual attempts by military officers and others to bring down Hitler's regime, the best is Peter Hoffmann, *The History of German Resistance, 1933–1945* (Cambridge, MA: Harvard University Press, 1977).

IV The Social Impact of Nazism

Two of the first efforts to evaluate the effects of Nazism on class structure and social status in Germany were David Schoenbaum, *Hitler's Social Revolution* (New York: Doubleday, 1966) and Ralf Dahrendorf, *Society and Democracy in Germany* (New York: Doubleday, 1967). These general essays have been supplemented by a host of monographs on specialized subjects, as these selected titles indicate: Timothy Tilton, *Nazism, Neo-Nazism, and the Peasantry* (Bloomington, IN: Indiana University Press, 1975); John Farquarson, *The Plough and the Swastika: The NSDAP and Agriculture in Germany, 1928–1945* (London: Sage Publications, 1976); Henry Grosshans, *Hitler and the Artists* (New York: Holmes and Meier, 1983); David Welch, *Propaganda and the German Cinema* (New York: Oxford University Press, 1985); and Alan D. Beyerchen, *Scientists under Hitler: Politics and the Physics Community in the Third Reich*, 2d ed. (New Haven: Yale University Press, 1985). An interesting attempt to apply computer techniques to social history is the work of Peter Merkl, *Political Violence under the Swastika* (Princeton, NJ: Princeton University Press, 1975).

Serious treatment of the youth movement began with Walter Z. Laqueur, *Young Germany: A History of the German Youth Movement* (New York: Basic Books, 1962). That has been followed by Peter D. Strachura, *Nazi Youth in the Weimar Republic* (Santa Barbara, CA: Clio Books, 1975); Geoffrey Giles, *Students and National Socialism in Germany* (Princeton, NJ: Princeton University Press, 1985); and Gilmer W. Blackburn, *Education in the Third Reich* (Albany, NY: State University of New York Press, 1985). Suggestive and controversial is the essay by Peter Loewenberg, "The Psychohistorical Origins of the Nazi Youth Cohort," *American Historical Review*, vol. 76 (December 1971), pp. 1475–1502, an excerpt from which is included in this volume.

The history of the German labor movement has not been fully treated in English. Perhaps the best single volume on the subject is by an Englishman, but it is available only in German: Timothy W. Mason, *Sozialpolitik im Dritten Reich* (Opladen: Westdeutscher Verlag, 1977). A bare outline is afforded in Mason's article, partially reprinted in this volume, "Labour in the Third Reich, 1933–1939," *Past and Present*, vol. 33 (1966), pp. 112–41. Background is provided by Max H. Kele, *Nazis and Workers: National Socialist Appeals to German Labor, 1919–1933* (Chapel Hill, NC: University of North Carolina Press, 1972).

In the field of women's history, two books can be especially recommended: Jill Stephenson, *Women in Nazi Society* (London: Barnes and Noble Books, 1975) and more recently, Claudia Koonz, *Mothers in the Fatherland: Woman, the Family, and Nazi Politics* (New York: St. Martin's Press, 1987).

Much scholarly attention has been devoted to the tragic history of Jews. Still indispensable as background are the volumes by Raoul Hilberg, *The Destruction of the European Jews* (Chicago: Quadrangle Books, 1961) and Peter C. Pulzer, *The Rise of Political Anti-Semitism in Germany and Austria* (New York: Wiley, 1964). Several more recent reconsiderations are original and thoughtful: Sarah Gordon, *Hitler, Germans and the "Jewish Question"* (Princeton, NJ: Princeton University Press, 1984); Martin Gilbert, *The Holocaust: The History of Jews in Europe During the Second World War* (New York: Holt, Rinehart and Winston, 1985); Detlef Peukert, *Inside Nazi Germany: Conformity, Opposition, and Racism in Everyday Life* (New Haven, CT: Yale University Press, 1987); Michael R. Marrus, *The Holocaust in History* (Hanover, NH: University Press of New England, 1987); and Charles S. Maier, *The Unmasterable Past: History, Holocaust, and German National Identity* (Cambridge, MA: Harvard University Press, 1988).